Entrepreneurial Women

—Book II—

by Colleen Perri

Possibilities Publishing
Kenosha, WI

Copyright © 1989 by Colleen Perri
Printed in the United States of America

Library of Congress Cataloging in Publication Data
   Perri, Colleen A.
   Entrepreneurial Women - Book II.
   Success Stories of Women Who Own Their Own Businesses.
   Bibliography: p. Includes index.
   1. Women-owned business enterprises - United States - Case studies.
   2. New business enterprises - United States - Case Studies.
   3. Women in business—United States—Case studies.
         I. Title
         HD2346.U5P434 1989 338'.04'088042   89-7370
         ISBN 0-941579-02-6

Acknowledgments

This book could not have been written and published without the cooperation and support of many people:

My husband Frank, who was always there whenever I needed him—whether to take pictures for the book, resolve a computer problem, make back-up copies of the daily drafts, or offer an encouraging word at the right moment—not to mention keeping the home fires burning so that I could enjoy the luxury of spending uninterrupted hours at my computer.

A quartet of talented editors: Suzan Kaye, Maureen Reed, Marcia Hodson and Linda Flashinski for correcting my grammatical idiosyncracies, tidying up my punctuation, and polishing my prose. Thanks also to Suzan for her excellent proofreading.

Once again Kathy Carson lent her talents to the cover design and made sure all the pictures were on straight.

And finally, the women who so graciously shared their special stories.

Introduction

My first book, *Entrepreneurial Women,* was intended to be a "Hometown Kenosha" seller. That's not how it turned out at all.

I was delighted when orders arrived from neighboring communities, and then flabbergasted when I began receiving letters from places like Salem, Massachusetts; Falls Church, Virginia; and even Cornwall, Ontario. Thanks to relatives and friends of the women featured in the book, it was traveling all over the country!

It soon became apparent that whether an entrepreneurial woman is from Kenosha, Wisconsin; New Foundland, New Jersey; or St. John, Missouri—the problems and challenges are the same: failure to be taken seriously as businessowners; automatic rejection by the majority of lending institutions; shoestring advertising budgets; and a race against the clock to cover home, family and the needs of a budding business.

Many women-owned businesses start at home base. Often she's the sole employee. Her knowledge of research, advertising, marketing, and financing is scant. Her needs are usually considered too miniscule to qualify for assistance from either the Small Business Administration or Economic Development Programs. It's been said that it's harder for a woman to acquire $5,000 to start a business than it is for a man to come up with $250,000 for a small factory. Yet, despite these many difficulties women are starting businesses in record numbers and, what's more, they are succeeding!

The 22 women profiled in *Entrpreneurial Women* are living proof that women are succeeding in business. I hope you decide to join them!

Table of Contents

Carol Dosemagen
Toys Again and Again

Toys Again and Again is a favorite stopping off point, not only for kids, but for grown-ups wanting to stretch their shopping dollars or turned used toys into quick cash. What's more, those used toys don't need to be in top-notch condition. Owner Carol Dosemagen and her husband Paul do all the cleaning and fixing. The only thing she doesn't buy often is stuffed animals. "I'm very fussy about those. They have to look and feel clean."

She adds, "If a toy is broken, I can usually make it whole

again." If not, she can always use the parts. The numerous bins, cabinets and drawers filled with spare parts are testimonial to this. Some drawers contain nothing but different-sized wheels. Others hold parts for games: Cootie, Dominoes, Bingo. She points out a dollhouse that would be perfect if the chimney weren't missing. "Eventually, one will come that we can use." She prides herself on selling only toys that are complete—including board games and puzzles. "I give my guarantee." Her children, who are paid on an incentive basis, have become experts at counting pieces.

Carol buys things outright, and uses Sears', Wards' and Penney's catalogs dating back to 1972 as guides for pricing. She finds the lowest price for an item and charges half of that. She also keeps an eye on sales at the stores at any given time and cuts her prices accordingly. "The only thing I don't do is give rebates."

At Toys Again and Again, it's possible to pick up toys seldom found on the market these days, such as electric football and basketball games. "They are sturdier than the newer plastic versions."

The possibility of discovering vintage toys draws many doll collectors to Toys Again and Again looking for finds such as "Tippy Toes," a doll who pushes a tiny stroller, Shirley Temples, and early Barbie dolls. "Anything Barbie is popular. Her pink Corvette is in big demand."

Carol maintains a waiting list to oblige collectors. In addition to doll collectors, there are always people seeking metal Jack-in-the-Boxes, model cars, and anything relating to T.V. shows of the forties, fifties and sixties. Fisher-Price play sets are popular, as are See & Say toys, and anything with a Little Tikes label.

Carol's career as "The Toy Lady" began after she read an article in *Woman's Day* magazine about a toy resale business. Trying to conceal her excitement, she asked her husband Paul, "What do you think about this idea?" When he said that he liked it, she was off and running.

She placed a classified ad in the local paper: *We buy unwanted toys. Any kind, any condition.* "The response was tremendous!" Carol remembers. Next, she began patronizing every rummage sale in town scouting for toys. Before long, there were toys in the basement, in the front room, in the bedrooms. "Toys were all over—our kids loved it!"

The Dosemagens originally planned to rent a building for Carol's shop. Then one day a ten-acre piece of property and home caught Paul's eye. He brought Carol to see it and, although they were in the midst of remodeling their own home, they purchased the real estate. They finished remodeling their original home, sold it and moved into their new home, where they embarked on a major program of painting and cleaning. "The house was so bad, I had to put plans for the business on hold."

Once the house was in order, Paul turned his attention to the large barn on the property. Built in 1912, the siding was loose, the doors were rotting and every window was broken. Paul was undaunted. A talented carpenter as well as an avid collector of "everything," he could see the storage potential of this 100-foot square barn. Suddenly, it dawned on him: *The store could be right there in the barn!* Carol agreed that it was perfect.

With the help of friends, Paul and Carol plastered, insulated, and painted. The only hired help came from an electrician who installed additional outlets. Paul built the counters and the handsome wooden staircase leading to the second floor where the shop is located. Carol says, "Without him, there wouldn't be a toy store." Shelves and several large bins were purchased and filled with toys and books. Life-sized decals of Goofy, Pluto, and other Disney characters provided the finishing touch, adding color and life to the white walls.

At 10:00 AM, on Tuesday, December 2, 1986, Toys Again and Again opened for business. "Was I nervous!" Yet the opening was greeted by eager parents and grandparents who trooped in and departed with grocery sacks filled with toys. "One lady was thrilled because she was giving a birthday party, and I had a whole bin of things marked three for a dime."

Carol credits a large part of her early success to considerable advance advertising in a free weekly advertising circular. "That really paid off." In addition to frequent newspaper ads, Carol also does direct mailings to new mothers. The hand-lettered pink and blue flyers contain detailed information about Toys Again and Again and offer a 10% discount on purchase prices. And she sends flyers to area nursery schools and day care centers. "They're always in the market for toys."

Carol has polished her marketing techniques along the way. For example, no one took a second look at the like-new baby rattles when they were heaped in a little plastic tub. Yet the same rattles went like hotcakes after she tucked each one into a see-through bag, stapled it closed, and attached a Toys Again and Again label. "Now I buy plastic bags in large quantities." Ironically, if adults prefer to buy packaged items, she says kids think it's great to get toys that don't require peeling off layers of wrappings. "They're in a hurry."

According to Carol the most difficult thing about the toy business is the amount of room required. "Space for riding toys is always filled to the max." She hopes that someday they can open up the entire top floor of the barn, which would triple the display space. "I'd love to set up electric trains and have special sections for different kinds of toys."

There are other minor headaches. For instance, "No one told us about the importance of checking out your business name in advance. We found out the hard way and it cost us a lot of money. We had to change our name, our stationery, business cards, everything." Also, after the Christmas rush, the winter months are slow. "I'm sure glad I'm not paying rent someplace." And there are always some people who quibble about the prices she pays for used toys. "Condition makes a big difference in the price I pay. People sometimes think their toys are more valuable than they actually are because they have attached so much sentimental value to them." In cases like these, she suggests the party place an ad in the paper and sell those items themselves.

While she says, she'll probably never get rich at it, Carol's toy business provides many satisfactions. Her kids love it. "Everybody's always anxious to help." Chris (13) excels at assembling MASK and Transformer toys (Carol says once they're apart, she can never get them back together again), Sarah (11) tends to Barbie and her fashions, Jacob (8) is in charge of G.I. Joe and his equipment, and Kenton (7) reigns over the Masters of the Universe. Carol says it's not unusual for the children to "borrow" something—sometimes for indefinite periods.

"It's pleasurable helping people. Where else can grandparents come in and really stock up on toys? People are so pleased when they can buy an expensive toy for half the price, or find something that's not made anymore. When I just happen to have a missing piece that's needed for a racetrack or something, it's very rewarding."

"You need to do lots of advance preparation—nothing can be done overnight. You <u>have</u> to be organized, because it's up to you if you make it or break it. If you can't spend a lot of money on advertising, it pays to take time to compare costs."

Carole Fogle
Youth and Family Services
Space Age Food Enterprises

Roget's Thesaurus describes an "entrepreneur" as a trier, hoper, tester, searcher, quester, striver, and fighter. If I had to select one woman from the many I have interviewed during the past two years who most reflects these characteristics, it would be the indefatigable Carole Fogle.

Once most people find a niche they are content to remain there, or if they branch out into other areas, they do so slowly. Slowly? That's not Carole's style. Once, she overheard two ladies in a restaurant powder room discussing "Life Call," a service for senior citizens. (By simply pushing buttons located by the bathtub, telephone or on a necklace, it's possible through Life Call to signal police and fire departments.) The fact that Carole happened to be "sitting in the john" at the time didn't stop her; by the time she left the powder room, she was in charge of developing a new sales force for Life Call.

Carole's other business endeavors include: Youth and Family Services, a counseling service for troubled families in the Kenosha area; Space Age Food Enterprises, a distributorship for Yurika Foods, which markets a line of convenience foods; and Interface Systems, Inc., a computer assessment service for psychologists.

Carole's first priority remains Youth and Family Services. This commitment evolved from a philosophical paper Carole and her psychologist husband, Dick, developed on the need for counseling family-related problems. Fortunately for the couple, Kenosha County's Comprehensive Board made a decision at about that time to develop a network of professionals for mental health services in the community. The Fogles sent their paper to the Board and were awarded a contract.

Originally teamed with several business associates, they soon bought out their partners. Today, they employ four full-time and five part-time licensed psychologists and social workers, in addition to two full-time bookkeepers, two part-time secretaries, and a once-a-week cleaning lady.

Youth and Family Services' first location was in a church basement, a site soon outgrown. For the next two years, it was located in a five-room house before moving to their current location in 1976. Ironically, they had purchased the building several years before as income property.

"We thought all we would have to do was put up a few walls." Before they were done, they had invested $12,000 in remodeling several bathrooms, installing air conditioning, tearing down an old garage and adding a gravel parking lot. Taking pains to avoid a cold, sterile atmosphere, Carole, Dick, and volunteer helpers placed carpet-like coverings on the walls. Not only did this provide the homey kind of atmosphere they wanted for clients, it also soundproofed the rooms.

Carole's office is decorated in earthy brown tones and orange accents. On the wall alongside daughter Renee's wedding pictures hangs a much-treasured plaque from a former client. Beautifully hand-lettered in calligraphy, it's a touching tribute to Carole. It was signed simply, "Your Friend."

Helping people to grow emotionally is her greatest reward,

says Carole. She describes her work as teaching people how to cope with life. "I liken life to an adventure story, and tell my clients that they need to get prepared for an adventure. I tell them they are going to learn about happiness, what the world is all about, and how to get along in that world."

Carole draws this analogy: "Each person has a backpack which they fill with facts as they go through life. Because we're going to be carrying it around with us wherever we go, we want to pack carefully. We have to be selective about what we put in it. A traumatic event can sidetrack us. It becomes a burden or a rock in our backpack. It's heavy and if we don't get rid of it, by the time we grow older, we're no longer standing straight. All we see is our feet. It's my job to help people take those rocks out of their backpacks, look at them and then throw them away."

Carole says that almost 80% of her clients are women suffering from anxiety and panic attacks. Some are incapacitated to the point that they are housebound. In such cases, she goes directly to the home to begin the activating process. "It's not long before they are motivated to leave the house."

Other clientele include people with problems related to raising children, marital discord, depression, drugs and alcohol. She says most aren't forward-looking people. "They look backward and feel hopeless. They have no burning desires; I have to teach them how to develop desires. They feel worthless; I have to show them their strengths. They particularly need help in goal-setting."

One way of implementing goals is using what Carole calls "mind expander exercises." "I ask them to imagine something they are going to accomplish that afternoon; then something they would like to accomplish the next day and then the following week and on from there." She finds this approach to be very effective with teenagers.

Although the agency satisfies Carole's professional needs, she says there are some drawbacks to her profession. "The results of our services aren't as tangible as those of a doctor who fixes a broken leg, etc. A person may feel significantly better and more able to cope with their problems because of our services, but how do you put a price tag on feelings?"

A stereotype prevails regarding people in social work: "As do-gooders our services should be free. People are surprised that Youth and Family Services is a for-profit agency. They don't realize it cost us $150,000 just to learn this business. When county funding decreased, our business suffered a large drop in revenue. We had to pump our own funds into it to keep going. We're still dealing with that. It has forced us to take a hard look at our business—that's when we became business people."

Ever the entrepreneur, Carole decided to sell computer assessment services to other psychologists after she and Dick designed a program to keep their own records, test results and services straight; thus, Interface Sytems, Inc. began.

Basement quarters at Youth and Family Services have been converted into a store for Carole's second—or is it third?—business, Space Age Food Enterprises. There she distributes a wide assortment of convenient gourmet meals from Yurika Foods including beef stroganoff, shrimp creole, and chicken breasts in wine sauce as well as "Phoenix for Life" weight control products.

Wooden shelves are lined with "complete protein" pastas, low-cal snacks, beverages, cookie mixes, and nutritious whole grain breads. Clients are often treated to the fragrance of baking bread.

Someone fixed an appetizing dinner for her in less than five minutes—that was enough to convince Carole to become a distributor for Yurika Foods . "Right away I could see the opportunity for people who are busy and yet want good quality food." She was also impressed with Yurika's multi-level marketing organization.

Carole named this business Space Age Food Enterprises because Yurika Foods was a developer of food products for the Space Program, and it's also a very forward-looking company. The acronym is S.A.F.E. "I wanted to bring out the fact that these products don't have any additives."

With a twinkle in her eye, Carole describes a recent advertising promotion, which involved purchasing a 1966 Cadillac hearse. After restoring the engine, the Fogles drove the car to California sporting the sign: *Don't die of preservatives—eat Yurika Foods.* "We took our CB along so that we could have conversations with people along the way."

Because she feels her products would be a boon to campers, Carole placed a three-month series of ads in *Sports Afield.* For $3, interested readers receive information and samples. She also rented a booth at a camper and boat show. "I demonstrated how easy it is to fix nutritious meals in a hurry. People appreciate the minimal clean-up."

15

Carole admits she revels in meeting new challenges. "I'm not a couch potato who lives vicariously all the time or is too timid to experience life and what it holds." She admits to being a risk-taker and an eternal optimist. "I look at an idea and am willing to try it. I'm not afraid of failure because I believe in the 'you can always make lemonade' theory."

Even as a child, Carole was a positive thinker. She was also precocious. As a toddler, she warbled *Away in a Manger* as a solo in a Christmas program at church in her hometown of New London, Iowa. "I had to crawl up the steps to get on the stage." By age three, she was reading, and by four, she was in kindergarten. She by-passed second grade when shifting was necessary to keep each grade occupied in the little country school.

Extremely active in high school—class plays, yearbook, basketball, marching band, French horn, coronet, bell lyres, and girls choir, where she often performed solo—she graduated at the age of 16. She also met her future husband during those high school years. "We were a street-corner romance. I was only 13 and he was 17, so we waited more than five years to get married."

Armed with a two-year provisional teaching certificate, Carole taught lower elementary school for four years, while Dick attended Bradley University in Peoria and earned degrees in English and Psychology. He went on to earn a Masters in Counseling while she completed her degree in Elementary Education. At the same time, the young Fogles, no strangers to hard work, also ran a boarding house for 16 college students. They developed a habit of saving a $25 bond per paycheck.

By the time time they graduated together from Illinois State University in Normal, Illinois, their only child, daughter Renee, had arrived on the scene. Carole went on to pursue her Masters of Education intending to become a school psychologist, while Dick earned his Ph.D.

Obviously, the Fogles are a well-matched pair. After attending school together, teaching school together, working as school psychologists together, and finally going into business together, Carole says, "We're still best friends."

Carole is a strong advocate of the women's movement. Although she had been the sole director of Youth and Family Services since 1980, when she applied at the bank for funding for computers she was told, "Bring your husband in and we'll talk."

16

She replied, "I'm the negotiator—not my husband." Then, she calmly picked up her purse and walked out. "I wrote them off and kept calling banks until I found someone willing to listen." When she did, she gave a 20-minute capsulization of her business plan and, although she had never had an account with that particular bank before, the banker was impressed enough to give her the necessary $50,000 loan.

Another milestone for Carole was being elected President of the Computer Based Assessment Association, a national corporation which is made up of 125 licensed psychologists and psychiatrists. (Carole is neither.) A founder of the three-year-old organization, she is the only female on its board of directors.

Carole served three years as an active member of the Kenosha County Planning and Budget Committee. "I put in hours of work making decisions on how to parcel out money." Because she was often told, "You are what we need in politics," she seriously considered a political career, until she worked on several campaigns. "The more I saw, the more I learned that political jobs are thankless."

Other activities include serving as a lobbyist for Wisconsin Association for Outpatient Mental Health Facilities, serving as a sustaining Girl Scout member, and belonging to Kenosha Women's Network.

Carole's various endeavors take 50-plus hours a week. That doesn't include her time spent loading firewood for Quality Wood Products, a firewood delivery business which Dick has been running for the past three years. Somehow, she manages to squeeze in leisure activities such as decorating their home with antiques. "I'm one of those people who should have a sign, *This car stops for garage sales*." Because Carole has reached the stage where she has more furniture than room, she has turned her attention to Victorian jewelry. "It's smaller. It's also easier to sneak into the house."

Goals for the future include making $20,000 a month with her Space Age Foods business. She's giving herself five years to do it. In a few short months, she opened a second store in Cedar Rapids, Iowa, which her sister, Joan Beardsley, runs. Recently she opened a third in Milwaukee.

Because computer-based assessment is growing in private practice in psychology, and because they have a leading edge in the area, Carole believes that Interface Systems has the potential to out-pace Youth and Family Services (business-wise) eventually. "However, our commitment to help others through Youth and Family Services will always play an important role in our lives."

Editor's Note: Shortly before this book went to press, Carole embarked on still another venture—Fogle and Associates Insurance Agency.

"Desire to be independent business-wise. Remember, no idea is a bad idea—all have merit. The smallest one can blossom. Network and bounce your ideas off someone else's. Listen and keep your ears open. Become as knowledgeable as you can by reading magazines like Entrepreneur. Not only read, also watch T.V. to find out what other people are doing. It will help you expand your horizons."

"You have to be a self-starter. People will try to discourage you, so your energy must come from within. There will be days when you will feel down. You have to pick yourself up, brush yourself off and say: 'So I got knocked on my can, but I learned.' Consider the experience a stepping stone—not a step back. If you have a negative attitude, I recommend associating with positive-thinking people before you attempt a new idea."

Elvia Fumo, Dora Marano & Carol Fumo
Sew Exclusive

Elvia Fumo always dreamed of becoming a dress designer; but, as a widow with seven children to support, she was forced to take whatever work she could find. The children grew up and, although she still desired a career utilizing her sewing skills, Elvia was hesitant. "I didn't know if I could handle the pressures of dressmaking, fittings and deadlines."

An idea took hold when she read an article about a woman who started a home-based business sewing heirloom-quality christening gowns and bridal accessories. "It sounded like a great idea for me!" She immediately tracked down the garter from her own wedding 36 years before. "It was in tatters. I thought how nice it would be to have had one in a lace that would have held up."

She shared her idea with the two family members who she hoped would become her partners—her daughter, Carol, and her sister, Dora. The three women, who enjoyed a common interest in crafts, once chipped in and rented a booth at one of the community's largest Christmas craft fairs. ("Kenosha had its biggest snow storm of the year that day, and we ended up giving most of our things away.") Elvia's enthusiasm for a new project was contagious and the women agreed to give the idea a try.

At first, they thought they'd concentrate their efforts on making christening gowns. They also considered making maternity clothes for career women. Elvia's oldest son, Rick, is an accountant who works with small businesses and is aware of the problems and pitfalls they encounter. He insisted they research the market. "He said we needed to find out if anyone would really be interested in our product and also if our workmanship was as good as everyone else's. We found out that ours was actually better!"

They made several christening gowns and learned that, while people acknowledged that the gowns were lovely, they were unwilling to pay the price. "That's when the idea of making bridal accessories really surfaced. The other ideas didn't appear to be cost effective."

Rick read about a woman in West Allis, Wisconsin, who made wedding accessories in addition to printing wedding invitations. Her business had doubled every year. He encouraged Elvia to visit that woman. "I was reluctant, but he kept nagging every time I saw him, 'Did you go yet?' So all three of us went." Encouraged by the woman's interest, the threesome hurried home and began making garters, pillows, hankies, and purses. When they returned, they had several hundred dollars worth of items. "When she ran to get her checkbook, we knew we had found our market!"

Elvia says that with Rick keeping an eye on things, they were forced to follow all the steps necessary to start a small business, including writing a complete business plan. "He made us put everything on paper—even our goals. He said, 'The more you do on paper, the easier it will be afterwards.' At the time, it took a lot of effort to make that extra push. Now we admit it was worth the trouble." In fact, they went a step further than most emerging businesses and developed a strong business philosophy: "Always to be honest in all of our transactions and do the very best work we possibly can."

Another first step was coming up with a name. First they put their names together and came up with "Elcador." "Because it sounded like a Spanish dancer, we decided to forget it in a hurry!"

They liked the idea of including the word "sew" in the title and considered "Sew Exquisite" before settling on "Sew Exclusive." It was Elvia's idea to use a dove in their logo. "It's a symbol of marriage and is also often used as a religious symbol. It just tied into the whole thing."

They decided on a home-based location after Rick advised against a store front. "He said it would be a headache worrying about insurance, staffing and shoplifting." Elvia then contacted local zoning authorities, and was closely questioned about the traffic her sewing business would bring into the neighborhood. "One of the reasons we decided to be manufacturers and sell directly to stores was that I didn't want a lot of people coming to my house."

Mondays and Tuesdays, Elvia, Dora, and Carol work together in an upstairs bedroom-turned-sewing-room, at Elvia's home. Each woman takes various projects home to work on during the week, and each has her own area of specialty within the group. Elvia tends to bookkeeping and ordering supplies. She also serves as chief navigator on selling trips to Chicago, Milwaukee, and locations between. Dora is the handwork expert. A floral designer by profession, she works magic with sequins and flowers. Dubbed the "hanky lady" because she is so adept at handsewing lace on handkerchiefs, Carol is also Sew Exclusive's official marketing representative.

At least twice a week, the striking Carol, who once considered a career as a make-up artist in a theatrical company, dons what she calls her "career outfits" (dark suit, white blouse, accenting jewelry, and high heels) and visits potential customers. She confesses she was scared when she made that premier sales call. "I didn't want to go in." Elvia, who drove her, says, "I had to give her a little pep talk outside the store." Since then, Carol has polished and fine-tuned her selling skills. "You just have to be friendly, honest, and low-key. It helps if you like people. At first, I had to gear up my courage, but that wore off when I saw people really liked our things."

Thanks in a large part to Carol's efforts, Sew Exclusive's items are now carried in 20 stores in Wisconsin, Illinois, and Michigan. Recently, she traveled to California and snared several hefty orders and is looking forward to an upcoming trip to Las Vegas.

One thing Carol learned early is not to make an appointment in advance. "It's too easy for people to say 'no' over the phone. But if I'm already in their store, they decide they might as well let me open my case."

Her smart-looking case holds garters in rainbow hues, stunning white and black satin and pearl bridal bags, satin ring bearer pillows in four different styles, and 100% Irish linen hankies. All decorations are sewn on by hand. "We don't use any glue."

Originally Sew Exclusive sold on consignment to a number of stores; now they rarely do. "There are just too many problems. You have to keep special records. People want to hang on to your things too long. Some bridal stores don't really have the space to display things, and it's no good having your things in a corner somewhere. We started with three stores on consignment: one did really well, one sold a few things, and one did zip. We learned that so much depends on the sales people. If they're enthusiastic about something, they'll move it."

Recently Sew Exclusive initiated a stepped-up advertising program. In hopes of tapping into the mail-order market, they are placing ads in *Modern Bride* magazine. And they are planning to mail 2,500 brochures to bridal stores throughout the country. They hired a designer in addition to a professional photographer to take pictures of a lace-trimmed hanky next to a rose for the brochure's cover. To obtain the desired pastel effect without paying for costly full color photography, they took advantage of a new color added-on technique. "It's great if you can't afford a four-color picture."

Elvia says the brochures not only represent their biggest capital investment thus far, they have also been Sew Exclusive's most expensive learning experience. "The printer didn't include the price of inserts in the original quote and then zapped us later with a huge bill. We had to sell lots of garters to pay for that oversight."

As with any new business, there have been growing pains because the bridal business is virtually dormant October through January. "Weddings don't come until after the first of the year." Sometimes an idea doesn't quite work out—like the black metallic purse which was to be trimmed with fringe, except no one had the fringe they needed.

Sometimes it's necessary to experiment with various materials for particular items before they stumble on to the right one. "We've learned to buy in small quantities because it's frustrating to have lots of leftover 'wrong' materials. It's easier now that we have more knowledge of the market. We know what sells and can make things ahead without having stock left over."

Elvia says they are proud of the fact that they now purchase everything at wholesale prices instead of retail. "That's a mark of the true professional."

Now that they have most of their designs perfected, the women are ready to proceed with other ideas. Elvia is taking classes on making hats and veils. "They are more profitable than what we are making right now, but there are so many styles . . . I guess you can say we are toying with ideas." They are also thinking of branching out from bridal stores to gift shops.

Elvia, Dora, and Carol all agree running a business is hard work. However, Elvia is quick to point out the advantages. "We like working our own hours. It's convenient working at home and it's nice to know people love what we make. Most of all, we enjoy what we're doing."

"Research! You need to find out if there's a market for your product. Often, people feel that what they make or write, etc., isn't good enough. That's not true. Keep sending your things out—someone along the way will like it."

Emilie Gerou
Technical Illustrator & Job Shopper

As a little girl growing up in Escanaba, Michigan, Emilie Sauvoy displayed a flair for art. When she was in kindergarten, she drew a picture of a dog, which the teacher immediately recognized as a poodle. "After that I had permission to use the poster paints and easel anytime I wanted." When she was in second grade she experimented with color combinations and was delighted to discover she could build up layers of fluid colors if she warmed her crayons in the sun. As a sixth grader, she became fascinated with gothic cathedrals and their stained glass windows. "I spent hours copying the central rose pattern until I wore holes in the paper with my compass."

After graduating from high school, she enrolled in college but she dropped out two semesters later when she ran out of money. Shortly afterwards, she entered what she ruefully describes as "a practice marriage" because the union lasted less than a year.

At that time she was living in Kenosha, Wisconsin, which

was going through a recession, and jobs were scarce. Emilie sold vacuum cleaners and magazine subscriptions, waitressed, and even tried a short stint in light industry. "It was a sweat shop." At last, she found a position with potential at Wisconsin Telephone. Hired as a switchboard operator, she soon was transferred to the night shift and greater responsibilities. "You had to know everyone's job." She moved to a Junior Supervisor position and a week later was elevated to a Senior Supervisor, where she remained until her marriage to Larry Gerou four years later.

The Gerous moved to Thorneville, a suburb outside of Newark, Ohio, where her husband worked as a systems analyst for Minuteman Missiles. Emilie settled in as a full-time mom who baked a dozen loaves of bread a week and raised her own produce. "I put in 50 cucumber vines and 150 tomato plants. It took us three months to can the vegetables!" When she wasn't canning, Emilie painted— or tried to—at least four hours a day in an upstairs bedroom-turned-studio.

Things didn't always go smoothly. On one occasion, a two-year-old daughter sampled the green oil paint off a jungle frond on a picture Emilie was painting. It was phtalacyanine and it took the Poison Control Center hours to get information about the chemicals. Finally, they had to call the paint company. Although the paint contained deadly cyanide, fortunately it was encapsulated. On another occasion, it appeared that one of her daughters sealed an eye shut with spray fixative. "Thank goodness, it was a false alarm. It turned out to be rubber cement, which she also got in her hair."

Emilie's full-time mom days ended when her husband was laid off in a major reduction in force at the base. Larry moved the family to Dayton, where he found another job. In order to supplement his income, Emilie took her first office job. "I soon learned that wasn't my thing."

An ad for a "mature woman to draw numbers on meter scales" captured her interest. "It sounded like a job for a little old lady with a paint brush." At her husband's urging, she went for an interview and learned the work involved drawing the entire scale on a hand-calibrated instrument scale using ink and a Leroy lettering device. "I decided to try it because the wages were decent and it looked like something I could do." She remained a scale technician until she was pirated away three years later by the larger corporation where her husband worked. Her wages doubled and she found a new challenge working with blueprints, isometrics, drawing and three-dimensional perspective, and electronic schematic diagrams. "These responsibilities required common sense and mechanical skills rather than mathematical abilities. I was never very good at math."

She was in her fifth year as a technical illustrator when President Nixon eliminated the capital investment credit which abruptly affected the gauging and control industry in which both the Gerous were working. "After the announcement was made, one-third of our company's standing orders were cancelled before noon." Her husband was laid off in October; Emilie in January.

To fill in the time until she could find a long-term position, Emilie took a "length of contract" job at Systems Research Labs doing documentation for AC-138E aircraft. It was here that she first heard of "job shoppers," people who take temporary positions in the technical illustrating, engineering, and computer programming fields. "I'd listen to them talk and thought it sounded interesting." She also learned that job shoppers earn a higher rate of pay per hour than a direct employee of the company. Unfortunately, job shopping involves constant travel—something unlikely for the mother of small children—so, Emilie put it out of her mind for the time being.

Instead, she found a position as a stripper and camera operator for a small weekly newspaper near their home. Not only was it enjoyable work, it also gave her the opportunity to do any draw-ings (maps, etc.) that were necessary. The skills learned there served her in good stead at her next position as Corporate Advertising Illustrator for Black Clawson Company in Middletown, Ohio.

Emilie describes her life during the next ten years as "frenetic." Not only was she holding a full-time, very responsible and demanding position, her family had increased to four children with son Steven's birth in 1974. At the same time, she was also a part-time student at Sinclair Community College in Dayton. Courses included a blend of the technical (air brushing, etc.) and purely artistic. "I was worried that my art work was becoming tight and constricted because I was spending so much time doing technical illustrations. I wanted to start thinking like an artist again instead of a mechanic."

Then, in 1979, Larry died suddenly, leaving her with three children ranging in age from five to fifteen. (Lenore, the oldest, already was on her own and living out of town.) A difficult period was made even more so when her father-in-law, a widower, was stricken with cancer and moved in with the family. She nursed him until he died in 1985.

When Steven reached junior high age, Emilie decided the time had arrived to attempt job shopping. In order to find possible positions, she turned to *Contract Engineer Weekly*, a national newspaper for job shoppers, which is arranged according to various skills as well as geographical areas. She learned that rates for assignments vary throughout the country: the Midwest runs the lowest at $12-$15/hour, while Texas offers the highest rate at $20. The East Coast falls somewhere between. Some companies offer a weekly living allowance (per diem) and travel expenses; others do not.

While the rate of pay may be higher than for positions as a direct employee, job shopping does have some disadvantages. "There is usually no sick time or any type of pension plan, although sometimes cooperative group insurance is available. Benefits such as holiday pay don't kick in until you've been with a particular shop for at least three months." She also learned that time worked for a company is cumulative: if you work for a company for two months and then are called back several months—even years—later, the original two months count as time already accrued.

One of her first major assignments was a three-month stint for Martin Marietta Aerospace in Baltimore. Because her car was in the repair shop at the time, she traveled to Baltimore via Amtrack. "I relished every single moment."

The travel Emilie thrives on doesn't appeal to everyone. She says it's not unusual for a job shopper to take a position as a direct employee of a company, choosing to give up the higher wage along with the constant traveling. Living for months in a motel room doesn't faze her. "As long as there's a secure lock on the door and locks on the windows, I can sleep through things that would probably bother someone else."

Although job shopping is predominantly a male-dominated field, Emilie says she has encountered very few problems because of her gender. She does recall the first day at a job where a young male technician remarked, "Oh good, now we have someone to make the coffee." She was delighted when her department head said, "Yes, she'll take her turn making it—just like the rest of us." She also learned it was automatically understood that a woman could never hope to be promoted to certain positions, such as ad manager.

She appreciates the rare camaraderie that exists among job

shoppers. "The exchange of information is great. They're very open about sharing information with each other—even if it means the other person will probably be competing for the same job. There's none of the pettiness that you usually find in the corporate world."

In addition to job shopping assignments, Emilie also does freelance art projects at home in her Cuckoo's Nest Art Studios (the name is borrowed from a line in one of Bea Lilly's songs, "If you ever ruffle up the feathers on a cuckoo's nest"). Most recent projects include illustrating *Growing Time*, a poetry book, as well as creating mastheads for several newsletters.

After long stints of working with isometric drawings, Emilie says that drawing people and flowers is a nice change of pace. "The two types of drawing are very different. In technical drawing, measurements prove if something is right or wrong. Other types of drawing are very subjective." While she enjoys the less technical drawing assignments, she says it can be a problem if a drawing has to be approved by a group. "As you know—it's hard to get a group to okay anything."

Another drawback to an art-related career is that the tools of the trade can be costly. "A set of pens can cost $300!" Emilie already has her next two investments in mind: an ultrasonic pen cleaner and a drafting machine. "That will be a tremendous aid for ruling and measuring angles." She also plans to take some computer graphics courses in order to expand the market for her services.

Other than that, Emilie says she's keeping herself open for whatever happens. "I don't want to know everything that's ahead. I hate being bored and having things too cut-and-dried. Insecurities don't bother me nearly as much as regularity does."

"Art has entered the computer age. In order to keep up in the field, you'll need to take computer graphics courses. Get that degree. It can make a difference of $10,000 a year in your salary."

Kathy Hermans
Cloud Nine Futons & Furnishings

Visions of soft, billowy fluffiness are conjured up in our imaginations upon hearing "Cloud Nine," the name of Kathy Hermans' mail-order business which specializes in children's futons and coordinating bedroom accessories.

Kathy and her husband Carl conceived the idea for this business when their son Andrew decided he outgrew his crib, but was still too small for the traditional twin bed. Having slept on futons themselves when they lived on Guam for three years, the Hermanses knew Andrew would be safe and comfortable sleeping on a futon right on his bedroom floor. (A futon is an all-cotton batting mattress that can be rolled up. It can be used on a frame that converts from couch to bed, or placed directly on the floor).

Even though Kathy was pleased over how well this idea worked out, she was also frustrated by her inability to find sheets and other bed coverings which would fit the futon and be attractive enough for a child's room. A talented seamstress who makes most of the family's clothing, including blue jeans, Kathy decided to create something herself.

One thing led to another and before long, the Hermanses found themselves in the business of making and selling futons along with pillowcases, comforters, drapes, bolsters and window shades in coordinating prints (they use the Gear Kids designs in 100% cotton fabrics), as well as zabutons (Japanese square floor cushions), buckwheat hull pillows (to provide extra support for neck and back), and yoga mats. Eventually, a line of play items including feltboards, fabric teepees and Batman and Superman capes would be added.

The decision to sell by mail order was made so that Kathy could stay home with Andrew while operating the business. She relates they spent almost a year planning. "We read everything we could find pertaining to mail order; ran some test surveys; made a rough draft of a catalog and possible mail-order ads and located sources for the materials we planned to use." They also made the decision to sell their home in Beloit, Wisconsin, and move to California, where Kathy's family resided.

The name "Cloud Nine" came to Kathy as most of our best ideas do; in the middle of the night. "I wanted a name that would evoke visions of cottony fluffiness and yet be clear enough to identify the product." The logo, a child snuggled fast asleep on a cloud, also represents this general concept.

In July 1986 Kathy obtained a business license, placed her first ad in *Mothering* magazine, and had a catalog printed. The first order was the direct result of an ad for the catalog. "The customer didn't even see the catalog itself! It was thrilling to know someone needed, wanted, and was willing to pay us for our product."

Kathy says most customers are parents of small children who want to solve a sleep need, such as the next step from a crib. Many are LaLeche League members who like the family bed concept, but need to enlarge the family bed space with a futon. "Some customers had already started decorating their child's room with Gear Kids and needed comforters, sheets, curtains, etc., to match."

Discovering and meeting the various laws and licenses pertaining to her business was a challenge. On one occasion they were informed by a label manufacturer that they would need a bedding license in order to make and sell futons. "We learned the definition of bureaucracy through experience. We also learned why many new businesses fail before they even open."

As with most mail-order businesses, its catalog was Cloud Nine's most costly item. Since the catalog is a mail-order's first, and often times only, introduction to the public, the Hermanses chose to go with a class act: glossy paper and full-color pictures. Savings were used to finance the project. "We wanted the customer to get an accurate idea of what the products looked like as well as how they would coordinate."

Son Andrew, a handsome little boy used to posing for pictures, willingly feigned sleep as he cuddled a red polka-dot pillow for the cover of the catalog. He is also pictured arranging shapes on one of his Mom's feltboards, playing a xylophone alongside a drum-playing teddy bear, and in feathered Indian headdress next to a Cloud Nine tepee.

Carl, a camera buff, did all of the photography. A financial planner, he assists Kathy in many phases of production, such as tying the quilts and mailing packages. He also provides essential feedback on ads and products, and cares for Andrew and the latest family addition, Christopher, when needed. "He's been very supportive of this venture."

She also credits her mother-in-law, Myrl Hermans, for playing a major part in Cloud Nine's success. "It is from her patient teaching that I learned how to do curtains and window shades. She also helped sew up items and man our booth at a baby show." She adds, "All the credit for the comforters goes to Carl's grandmother, Theresa Kressin, who passed on the art of hand-tied wool-filled comforters to anyone in the family who could tie a knot."

Kathy, formerly a music teacher, drew on her educational background to produce the catalog's explanatory text on the history of futons, directions for caring for them, as well as a section on futons and children. Among the advantages listed are: no more worry about the child falling from a crib or bed, and the easy portability which makes them perfect for sleepovers. This same portability also provides extra play space when needed. Finally, if the child is accustomed to sleeping in Mom and Dad's bed, a futon in the same room is a great next step into his or her own bed.

Kathy remembers that after the catalog was printed, they came up with additional project ideas. Rather than printing an entirely new catalog, they simply developed a price/product sheet which can be easily removed and replaced with updated versions each time the catalog is mailed out. "This way we can use all the catalogs on hand before going into a new printing."

Kathy feels the most successful avenue for advertising for Cloud Nine has been the national magazine, *Mothering*. They also had good success showing their line in baby shows at the Los Angeles and Anaheim Convention Centers. "This gave us an opportunity to show our products as well as talk with our customers." She adds that this contact resulted in several substantial orders.

According to Kathy, the business is now at the point where its cash flow meets all its needs and expenses, which no longer makes it necessary to borrow from family savings.

Kathy's workload varies depending on how many orders need to be sewn up. With the addition of son Christopher to the family, work time is usually limited to his nap times or those times he and Andrew are content to play by themselves. "When the orders start to pile up, then Carl and I go on overtime. We're both up until 2:00 AM hand-tying the comforters."

Plans for expansion are in the future because, with two active little boys, time to work on the business is limited. But that doesn't stop Kathy from making plans. "Some day I'd like to work with interior decorators, bedding and linen stores, and baby and children's shops. I have lots of ideas."

She sums up by saying she and Carl are as excited about their idea as the day it came to them two years ago. "It's so workable and the prints are so attractive. We're proud of our business. The centuries-old futon tailored to babies and children—that's unique."

For a copy of Cloud Nine's catalog, write:

Cloud Nine Futons & Furnishings
142 Loma Alta
Oceanside, CA 92054

"The hardest part is pricing and making decisions on how many dollars to spend on advertising. There are a lot of hard decisions to make and hard work, but along with that is a corresponding amount of personal growth and the satisfaction of setting new goals and learning new skills."

"If you are considering going into the mail-order business, read everything you can on advertising and writing copy. Study existing ads that have proven to be good sellers. Survey lots of people to see what their key reponses on your product are. That can also be helpful in creating a good headline and ad copy."

Jackie Hoffman
The Wool Shed

It all started with a 4-H project and three orphan lambs, "Fluffy," "Buffy," and "Lola." Jackie Hoffman decided it would be nice if she made something out of the wool for her children, Jodi, Jared, Joel, and Jayme. It took two years to find a teacher, but it was worth the trouble—Jackie took to spinning like the proverbial duck to water. "Arts and crafts are in the family genes. My mother is a wonderful knitter, and my sister, a talented painter."

When the original sheep went off to market, Jackie missed having her own source of wool; thus, "Ma Sheepy" and daughter "Patsy" entered their lives. Jackie knew her husband, Norman Clausen, would be upset. Not only had she paid an extravagant price for the new sheep, who were nothing but skin and bones (sadly neglected, they had been surviving on bread); but, more importantly, Norman, like his father before him, is a cattleman.

Jackie was all too aware of the long-standing animosity between cattlemen and sheepherders. "Sheep have a bad reputation for ruining fertile land because when they graze, they eat *everything*, including the roots." Deciding to keep the sheep a secret from her husband, she hid them in the barn. Her plan was quickly foiled when the undernourished sheep went into shock as soon as they were placed on an ordinary diet, requiring intensive care by a veterinarian. Soon she was forced to confess. "How else could I explain to my husband why I was meeting the vet out in the barn all the time?"

In one of those spur-of-the-moment decisions, Jackie says she went from "sheep to shawl." After raising the sheep, shearing their wool, cleaning it, dying it, spinning it into yarn, and weaving the yarn into cloth, it seemed logical to also sell it. Three days after the idea struck, she opened The Wool Shed at a new mall in her hometown of Kenosha. "I liked the tourist-type setting."

There wasn't a ceiling yet, so she taped up wallboard; there were no lights, so she found a friend to drop some in; the floors were bare, so she ordered carpeting and took anything she could get. She snatched a counter out from under another friend, stuck apple crates on the walls to hold her yarn, and was the first tenant in the mall ready for opening day, despite the fact that the others had started months before. That's Jackie. In fact, she even found time to help distribute bratwurst at the mall's combination Grand Opening/ OctoberFest celebration.

Actually, Jackie is no stranger to store openings, having worked at a retail clothing business for three years. During that time she moved up the ladder from clerk to assistant manager to manager to district manager. "I was fortunate to have a boss who shared everything involved in opening a store." He also taught her how to deal with people and buy wisely. Her two-year degree in Accounting also proved to be helpful.

Jackie says her original idea was to "sit and spin and tell people about wool." Response was tremendous. When there were too many people to fit into the little 100-square-foot shop, she merely moved her spinning wheel out into the open hallway.

When it became apparent that she couldn't squeeze in one more ball of yarn, Jackie moved to Simmons Plaza on Kenosha's south side. Although she gained more than 700 additional feet, she reports it was rapidly filled with sweaters, shawls, scarves, blankets, vests, hats, sheepskin slippers and gloves, knitting bags, afghan kits and a variety of finished and unfinished spinning wheels, to say nothing of the yarn—alpaca from Peru, cotton from Norway and mohair from England, Italy and Spain. "Before I knew it, I had things stacked as high as they could go." Jackie admits she doesn't take a wage. "I keep putting it right back into the shop—I always see more I want to buy."

The Wool Shed is teeming with sheep-related memorabilia: stained glass lambs, ceramic lambs wearing bright red mufflers, and fat wooly sheep embroidered with "I Love Ewe." Decked out in a white collar and pin-striped tie, E. F. Mutton is displayed in a box labelled "Preferred Sock." A copy of *The Wool Street Journal* hangs on the wall.

The sheep theme also overflows into her home. "Every celebration seems to bring a sheep-related gift with it." There are sheep figurines from India, Greece and Italy, collectors plates, coffee mugs and aprons—even wallpaper with a sheep motif. Not only that, now family and friends are flooding her with spinning wheel memorabilia.

Jackie's schedule isn't for the fainthearted. A typical day begins at 5:00 AM when she feeds the dairy herd. She helps start the milking and serves as an active member on the "poop" committee. Then at 6:30 AM, it's off to see the sheep, who are housed three miles down the road from the family farm. Her sheep work involves feeding, watering, and checking to see if everyone is okay. "I give love pats. We chat and discuss world politics." Not bad for a city gal who married into the farm life. She says she's always been the out-doorsy type, fond of animals and gardening. "I love it."

The pace picks up during lambing season, which runs from December to March. Jackie describes it as a totally hectic time with very little sleep. "I'm on call every four hours." Often, with long johns under her housecoat (at that time of the year, temperatures hover near zero), she assists with deliveries. "You always worry when it's the first time." Sometimes she has to make formula and bottlefeed lambs who are under-sized or orphans. "These lambs think I'm their mother and follow me around—even when they are older."

Another bustling time is October when Jackie shears the sheep. "I do it then so they'll fit better in the barn for winter. Since each sheep is wearing about 22 pounds of wool, that's quite a bit of space." An additional job is combing and washing thousands of pounds of oily, dirty wool.

There's lots of shearing because currently they have 150 sheep. "Patsy" is still there, but after ten years, "Ma Sheepy" quietly slipped away in her sleep. "I felt like I lost a friend." Present sheep include "Bent Ear," "Poke-E-Dots," "Cookie Monster"(chocolate chip cookies are his passion), "Itchy-Butt," and twins, "Victor and Victoria." At first, Jackie says, her family tried to name each sheep according to its personality characteristics. "We ran out of names."

Most are working sheep who earn their keep—either producing wool or serving as delicious roasts at Greek and Lithuanian festivals. Jackie admits she also runs sort of a retirement home. "After seven years of producing babies, I think my girls should be able to live out their lives peacefully. I wouldn't think of slaughtering them."

Most days, Jackie's at the Wool Shed by 10:00 AM. Throughout the day women stream in asking advice on spinning wheels, repairing sweaters, or what kind of yarn to use for a particular project. Some bring in their dog's hair to be spun into yarn for a hat, scarf, or a pair of slippers. "It's like having a piece of Fido around after he's gone." Others bring in hair from their long-haired cats. "Sometimes, all they want is a little ball of yarn to go in a basket with wooden knitting needles."

When not tending to customers, Jackie spins—blankets, shawls, and sweaters to use as samples in the shop. It can take six to eight hours at the spinning wheel to complete an item. "That's why I have the most powerful right leg in the city."

Three evenings a week during the winter months, she holds knitting, spinning, and weaving classes. Classes are purposely kept small (three to four people) so that she can give individualized instructions. "Weaving, especially, is very intricate. Often my students are concerned they'll make mistakes. I tell them, 'We don't make mistakes here. You're creating character.' "

Although Jackie says that she eats, dreams and sleeps Wool Shed, she manages to find time to run a small mail-order service which ships raw wool all over the United States. She also belongs to numerous associations: Kenosha Women's Network, because she believes it's essential for women in business to pull together; the National Wool Growers Association, which promotes American wool to the American people; and the National Black Sheep Wool

Growers, a group whose efforts are largely responsible for the fact that black sheep are finally recognized and now have their own shows at local, county, and state fairs. "Any sheep that's not white is considered 'black' and an outcast because its wool can't be dyed—therefore, it isn't versatile. Our group points out you never have to worry about black wool fading."

Obviously a virtuoso at time management, Jackie also takes an active part in the Black Sheep Spinners "Spin In," a yearly event featuring speakers, workshops, displays, contests, and a—what else?—lamb lunch. She also participates in Simmons Plaza's many joint advertising promotions. Her lamb and calf petting zoo is a featured attraction at Plaza events.

Jackie doesn't wait for special occasions to set up her spinning wheel outside. If it's nice, she's out there. "People always stop to watch." Whenever possible, she also places tables of sale items outside. Jackie says she's always trying to conceive ideas to attract attention to the shop.

Thus far, she has been the subject of articles in the *Chicago Tribune's* "Tempo" section and *Craft and Needlework* Magazine's "Retailer of the Month" column, as well as featured in numerous articles in local newspapers.

It's not always necessary for Jackie to seek out the press—sometimes it seeks her out. For example, a customer from Chicago mentioned Jackie and her sheep at a bridge party. One of the bridge players passed on the story to her husband, who happened to be a writer for the *Chicago Tribune.* "I think he was expecting this crazy lady in a prairie dress and bonnet smoking a corn cob pipe, and was surprised that I was halfway modern." His story led to coverage by CNN and exposure over national television. "I haven't had a chance to catch the show myself, but apparently lots of people have. Suddenly I'm taking orders for sheep over the phone!"

Paid advertising consists of monthly ads in all area papers as well as in *The Country Peddler,* a circular on collectibles, antiques, hobbies and crafts distributed by the Spinning and Weaving Guild. "You need to keep your name out there."

Jackie concedes she is looking forward to the day when she can hire help. Right now, when she takes a day off, she closes the shop. "The problem is, while anyone can sell yarn, it's hard to find someone who can warp a loom or give advice on which mordant to use for specific fibers. Guess I'll have to advertise for a spinner/weaver and see what happens."

Editor's Note: Just before this printing, The Wool Shed moved to a twice-as-large location at a new upscale mall in the Kenosha area.

"Have fun and enjoy what you're doing. Everyone's afraid to fail. Don't be afraid to dive in. If you fall on your face, too bad. If things don't work out the way you planned initially, don't sit down and cry. Pull up your socks and go again."

Chris Isham
Hearts 'N' Flowers

Whenever I teach a course on starting a small business, I'll have at least one student in the class who'll wistfully state she'd love to start her own business; unfortunately, it just isn't possible while her children are still at home. I'd like to introduce women like her to Chris Isham. When Chris kicked off Hearts 'N' Flowers, her floral and antique business, five years ago, she had nine children at home ranging in age from nineteen all the way down to eight. She also had two teenage stepchildren.

Instead of spending time away from their mom, who puts in more than 40 hours a week at her business, the children join her there. They answer the telephone, make bows, mix potpourri and do whatever else they're told. Chris reports they work well together.

A picture of relaxed confidence and bustling cheerfulness, Chris reflects her environment. "The kids in our family were encouraged to grow. My father always told us: 'Go ahead—try it.' " Then too, the family was grounded in a strong religious foundation. "One of my mother's key phrases was: 'If you don't go to church on Sunday, you won't get anywhere.' " One of the first things Chris did when opening Hearts 'N' Flowers was to dedicate it to St. Theresa, the saint known as "the Little Flower of Jesus."

Armed with a nest egg (earned through years of factory work and bartending duties), a "this is going to make it" philosophy, and lots of inspiration from her sister Dolli (who had six years experience as a floral designer), Chris plunged in where others would have feared to tread. Because of the immense inventory required, it takes a minimum of $25,000 to launch a floral business. An example of Hearts 'N' Flowers' shoestring budget: when they opened, they boasted a total of ten mylar balloons in stock. Now they carry more than 200 different choices, including full-size and miniature heliums for every occasion.

For Chris, a more pressing concern than stocking her shop was finding the right location. Although rent in the downtown open-air mall was affordable, it was a well-known fact around town that more than a few downtown stores had closed. "People kept telling me 'You won't make it down there.' So I had members of the family take turns sitting on a bench on the mall and count the number of people passing by." Chris was pleased to observe that a number of area businesses appeared to be doing surprisingly well.

The informal survey proved to be accurate, and Hearts 'N' Flowers enjoys frequent walk-in traffic. "People were pleased to have a floral shop downtown again. There hasn't been one in the district for more than 15 years. "

Not everything, Chris adds, has worked according to plan. She discovered that belonging to a wire service didn't pay for her. "It was a real rat race and required a sizable investment. You either break even or you lose." At one time, she considered offering a line of fancy candles. "It was 'no go' because the minimum investment would be $20,000."

"Opening Day" came and went several times. For one reason or another, Chris and Dolli kept postponing it until Chris firmly put her foot down and announced, "We're opening tomorrow" and made them stick to it. Tense and anxious, they admitted to being greatly relieved when it turned out to be a quiet day. When they finally felt reasonably settled, almost a month later, they celebrated an "official" Grand Opening Day. "Things went very nicely. We ran lots of ads ahead of time announcing we were giving away free flowers and balloons."

Originally, Hearts 'N' Flowers was predominantly flowers. Today, it's a pleasant mix of flowers and antiques, thanks to mother, Monica Gianakos, a long-time antique dealer who once owned an antique store. Alongside the fresh and potted flowers, grapevine wreaths, hanging pots, and baskets are pieces of vintage furniture, collectible china and bisque dolls, art deco clowns, and antique jewelry. For those charmed by the past, there are Dolly Dingle tie-ons and mailers, and Victorian boxes, bags, calendars, valentines, and lithograph prints.

Providing outstanding service is as important to Chris as her products are. "I want our customers to have complete satisfaction. If the roses don't open, I replace them." She recounts the time a customer wistfully mentioned she wished her roses were a slightly paler shade of pink. "I remade the entire bouquet. Since then, we've handled the flowers for two more weddings for that particular family." Chris went on to say that perhaps the greatest compliment to Hearts 'N' Flowers is the fact several floral designers are regular customers.

"I've been in too many places where they throw a book at you and expect you to choose what you want from a picture. Here, we use a color wheel, show actual samples and make suggestions. "That's really appreciated because it's easy for excited or nervous brides-to-be to forget things."

In addition to custom-tinting flowers and dyeing ribbons, making up the toss-away bouquet and garter, Hearts 'N' Flowers' services for weddings include: pinning flowers on special guests as well as the men in the wedding party, showing the bridesmaids the proper way to hold their flowers, and pointing out where guests of the bride and groom are supposed to sit in church. Equally comprehensive services are provided for funerals.

The 24-hour telephone service offered by Hearts 'N' Flowers is popular, as is the rental service which offers baskets, vases, silk floral arrangements, a wishing well, and a flowered trellis.

Both Chris and Dolli work full-time in the shop. As sole proprietor, Chris makes the major monetary decisions and handles the necessary bookwork, while Dolli is recognized as the chief designer. Decisions regarding advertising and decorating the shop are made jointly. "We consider our windows an essential part of our advertising program." The relatively unhurried periods after holidays and June weddings are welcome because they offer an opportunity to decorate the windows and develop new ideas as well as catch up on the cleaning.

Traveling on the job isn't out of the ordinary for the on-the-go sisters. They have journeyed to Nashville and Reno, among other places, where they stay for several days creating silk flower corsages and fresh flower arrangements for the annual "Shipmates Reunion" banquets for the retired Admiral and crew of the U.S.S. Brush (1943-1969). In these cases, they purchase fresh flowers from shops in the area, but do the arranging themselves.

Another particularly noteworthy experience was decorating an antique-filled yacht with greenery and solid brass. "There was even a grand piano on board. It was something else!"

When not busy with the shop, Chris is caught up in the myriad of activities a large family entails. Dolli, who is single, confesses to possessing an infatuation for sofas and buys a new one every year. As for Chris, she prefers new cars, and her floral shop helps pay for them.

"There's more hard work than glamour in this business. The hours are long and you'll never have perfect nails again."

"For a woman who wants to start a business, I say: 'Take the plunge and go for it.' Lots of people have great ideas, but then they don't follow through. If you don't try, nothing will ever happen."

Mercedes Kelly
Kelly Health Enterprises

At the age of 32, Mercedes Kelly had it all: A happy marriage, two "perfect" children, a lovely home and a job she loved. "You could say I was coasting through life on Cloud Nine." Then, one day, without warning, her cozy little Cloud Nine vanished into thin air.

It began with a mild stroke, which sent her to the hospital for four days. She was discharged, only to suffer a massive stroke a few days later. This time her entire left side was paralyzed.

"I always believed you could do anything you wanted if you wanted it badly enough, but I soon learned that once your brain cells are dead, they don't come back to life." There were other disturbing discoveries as well. When she smiled, one side of her face obeyed and curved up, while the other side turned down. An x-ray technician casually pointed to Mercedes' x-rays and then to another set which she described as *normal*. "That was the first time I realized I was no longer considered normal."

Although intensive therapy reduced much of the paralysis, Mercedes was left with residual spasticity, or a form of involuntary cramping. The result: A left hand that looked deformed. "That was hard to accept. I was very self-conscious about it and tried to hide my hand. When I saw pictures of myself, the first thing I looked at was my hand. I was always concerned about how spastic it might appear."

She was forced to come to grips with the fact that her stroke was a life-changing experience when she was forced to make the painful decision to resign from her "dream job" as a court reporter, which she had enjoyed for 11 years. Verbatim reporting requires speed in excess of 200 words a minute—something that was no longer possible with a spastic hand. (In recognition for her work in court reporting, Mercedes was named the First Honorary Member of the Wisconsin Shorthand Reporters Association.)

"What happens when you have the world by the tail and then something cuts off the tail? An optimistic person by nature, I decided I was lucky to still have the things that mattered most— a loving husband, my children, and a chance to live."

Determined to find another niche, Mercedes embarked on what she describes as her "periennial student" saga. Before she was through, she earned a degree in Accounting/Personnel at the University of Wisconsin-Parkside in Kenosha, as well as Associate Degrees in Secretarial Science, Licensed Practical Nursing, Marketing, and Horticulture Production. ("Taking that one was really worth it because, before I took the course, my huband wouldn't even allow me to water the garden.")

Mercedes was still betwixt and between when fate stepped in with an invitation to attend a Shaklee demonstration at a friend's home. She went because she was a long-time admirer of Shaklee's cleaning products. "That night I learned the body can't get everything it needs from food, and that through taking the proper food supplements, blood pressure can be lowered, and the risk of strokes, heart attacks, and cancer can be reduced considerably." Impressed, she decided to try some of the food supplements.

The resulting improvement in her health led to a heightened interest in nutrition which prompted her to enroll in a correspondence course in nutrition through the College of Nutripathy in Scottsdale, Arizona, which led first to a B.S. as a Professional Certified Nutritionist and then an M.S. in Nutripathic Science. She is currently in the Doctoral Program.

At the same time, Kelly Health Enterprises just kind of evolved. "I eased into it." The name was selected because she liked the acronym *Khe*. "I stumbled onto it quite by accident. I thought to myself, 'How appropriate—it's the key to good health; the key to my future; the key to success.' " A gold key bearing the message: *Your key to good health* is imprinted on her business cards and stationery.

Her office, previously her sewing room, reflects Mercedes' well-ordered personality and positive thinking. There's an IBM selectric typewriter, a calculator, and racks filled with literature and tapes on fitness, health, salesmanship, self-image and motivation. She believes tapes like "Born to Win" and "A Richer Life Course" can help people see themselves as truly successful by showing the steps it takes to get there. On the wall, a stained glass plaque with Robert Schuller's "Possibility Thinkers Creed" hangs next to a poster reading, "Are you sick and tired of being sick and tired?"

As soon as her stationery was printed and a business checking account opened, Mercedes says she immediately began prospecting for people interested in individual nutritional counseling and Shaklee products. Leads furnished by friends proved to be her most effective marketing tool. Additionally, she advertises in the printed programs for various events in Kenosha as well as in all local newspapers. She briefly utilized part-time telemarketing assistance, but felt the results didn't warrant continuing. Someday she hopes to place a listing in the *Yellow Pages*.

Mercedes particularly enjoys the flexibility a home-based business offers. "There isn't any clock to punch—there's no pressure." On the job approximately 20-25 hours a week, she readily admits she enjoys time off to travel with Bill (her husband of 30 years who recently retired from Chrysler Corporation) to visit their time-sharing units in Bella Vista, Arkansas, and the Bahamas.

Equally important, her free time enables her to play an active role with the Kenosha Chapter of the American Heart Association. She presents heart-healthy programs to local organizations and also speaks to area restaurants about heart-healthy dining, and is in the process of publishing a guide listing local restaurants which provide modified menu selections.

Mercedes' hours also afford time to participate in numerous professional organizations. Presently, she is a Board Member and Treasurer of Wisconsin Women Entrepreneurs, a member of Kenosha Women's Network, and Wisconsin Business Women's Coalition. She believes belonging to such groups is vital for women. "We learn from each other and there is also strength in numbers. It also leads to personal fulfillment, which I feel is the ultimate prospecting tool." In order to broaden her listening and leadership skills, she also belongs to a Toastmasters Club and currently serves as its president.

The flexibility which is such a plus, Mercedes points out, can also be a minus. "It's extremely easy to get sidetracked—I've developed the ability to procrastinate. When I don't push, I sometimes feel guilty. I know that I could be lots more serious about the hours I put in.

"Money isn't the main thing for me. My greatest reward is having people come back and say how much better they feel and look. They also enjoy saving money in the process."

On her desk sits a model of a tiny Mercedes, a gift from her children when she graduated from the University of Wisconsin-Parkside. "I always wanted a Mercedes so they made one for me." Daughter Valerie (Mrs. Gary Ludlow, "Mom" to the Kelly's first grandchild, Philip Roy), and son Glen, a student at the University of Wisconsin-Parkside, are understandably proud of their mother's many accomplishments.

"Scrupulous recordkeeping is necessary for those home-based business tax write-offs. Document everything. Develop a strong self-image. Rise above criticism; otherwise you're never going to make it."

Portrait by McDermott's Photography

Melody Kraai
Maple Ridge Adult Day Care Center

She once took a vocational test and scoffed when results indicated she would be best-suited to a nursing career. Melody Kraai says, "That was the last thing I wanted."

Later, she relented and enrolled in a six-week Nurse's Aide course offered at a local technical school and was surprised when she discovered she loved it. Shortly afterward, she found a job at a geriatric nursing facility. It was less than an auspicious beginning: the day she started, the staff went to lunch at noon and never returned; instead, they embarked on a month-long strike. "I got my feet wet real fast!"

In short order, Melody completed a Licensed Practical Nurse program, re-met and married Jim Kraai (who grew up in Melody's neighborhood), became Mom to a son, Aaron, in January 1979, followed by Adam in May 1980. She also continued to work full-time at the nursing home until baby Adam's predisposition to upper respiratory problems, some serious enough for hospitalization, led to her resignation.

Melody says of the short interval when she did babysitting in her home: "I grew tired of that in a hurry." Because she missed her work with the elderly, she took the first of several part-time positions at nursing homes. In each case, the part-time hours gradually expanded to full-time and more. "I worked second shift and if the third shift replacement didn't show up, I'd have to stay through the next shift. " Guilt-ridden because she was away from home so often, Melody would resign once again. Finally she settled in at a nursing home where the hours were predictable; then the management decided to eliminate all LPN positions.

The idea of an adult day care center emerged after Melody read about a woman in Milwaukee, Wisconsin, who was taking care of the elderly in her home. "The idea appealed to me because I became very attached to some of the seniors and used to bring them home with me for short visits."

Upon contacting the Department of Regulations and Licensing for Wisconsin, Melody learned it wasn't necessary to obtain a special permit. (That is now in the process of changing.) A call to the Department of Aging confirmed there was an enormous need for adult day care programs.

Contacts with both the Wisconsin Adult Day Care Association and the National Association proved to be turning points for Melody. "They were very helpful and supportive." She also received advice and assistance from the Village Church, a day care center in Milwaukee. "They shared all the forms they were using— all I had to do was change the letterhead. They also shared their tax reports. That helped make everything more concrete, more real."

The most difficult part of starting her own business was obtaining financing, says Melody. "It was discouraging." She approached the Small Business Administration for a loan and learned if it cost her three-quarters of a million dollars to build a facility, she would have to first come up with ten percent of it herself. "I didn't have that kind of money!"

Next, she visited local banks. Two refused loans almost before she opened her mouth; another listened and then claimed the idea was so *new* they couldn't consider it; still another denied a loan because it would be too risky—Melody didn't possess enough business experience. Even when her father, Roy Curio, who was well-known in the community as a businessman, stated he was willing to back her up, it wasn't enough.

Undeterred, Melody turned to Kenosha's Economic Development Corporation where Development Specialist Cecilia Lucas connected her with the Small Business Investment Corporation. For the first time, there was a glimmer of hope. SBIC had money targeted for minorities, were willing to lend $80,000, and back it 100%. Soon she found herself enmeshed in paperwork. "It was extremely involved. They always wanted 'just one more thing.' "

When she wasn't struggling with paperwork, Melody was looking for a suitable location, no easy task because of regulations regarding doorways, fire exits and wheel chair accessibility. Buildings in outlying locations were also ruled out because day care centers must be community-based. She finally found an empty school building which looked promising, only to have someone outbid her.

Then catastrophe—three days before the closing papers were to be signed, she received a call from SBIC. They were backing out. "I was sick." Fortunately, both her money and location dilemmas were solved when Ce Lucas suggested Melody talk to a local bank regarding a restaurant which was involved in bankruptcy proceedings. Although the bank was one of those that originally denied Melody a loan, this time they were willing to listen. "I was able to convince them there was a definite need for an adult day care program in the community."

The bank agreed to grant her a straight conventional loan if she pared $180,000 from her remodeling and equipment budget. Luckily, extensive remodeling was unneeded because the building was already wheelchair-accessible and possessed the necessary restrooms. Melody's husband, father and friends erected several walls and installed a new floor, as well as special equipment that was needed.

The building features a dining room, and a spacious activities room, where people can work on arts and crafts, exercise on a bike, listen to informative lectures, or enjoy live entertainment from visiting groups, such as Seegers Senior Strings or the Royalaires. A "quiet" room offers a fireplace, comfortable sofas and recliner chairs, an aquarium, and a large screen television set where old Douglas Fairbanks movies are particular favorites.

Maple Ridge Adult Day Care Center is named after a row of maple trees on Melody's originally selected site. "Those trees really stuck in my mind. Whenever we plant a new tree now, it will be a maple." Maple trees also constitute Maple Ridge's logo, which was designed by Melody's sister, Mona and her husband Tom McDermott, who are both professional photographers. Maple trees are also featured on the sign in front of the building and on the facility's van.

When she began hiring help, Melody's first consideration was experience working with the elderly. "I wanted people who enjoyed that kind of work." The staff boasts a total of 39 years of geriatric experience among them and includes a full-time LPN, two certified Nursing Assistants, and a combination Maintenance Man/Groundskeeper/Van Driver. Husband Jim also assists with the maintenance. "He's my main support in everything."

Maple Ridge offers an individualized plan of care to meet the needs of each participant. Services rendered include: supervision; medical and social evaluation; group and individual activities; health screening; exercise; personal and health care; meals; socialization; transportation; reality orientation; and medical and social services as needed.

Since it opened in January 1987, the number of regular participants in Maple Ridge's program has steadily increased. Melody considers educating the public an ongoing challenge. "I need to help the elderly person's caregivers realize they need to give themselves some time and space—that they need a day or two a week for themselves. So often they have the idea they should do everything at all times (24 hours a day) for the person. They have a lot of guilt if they don't."

Because she looks forward to the day when she'll no longer get calls from people who are interested in "child" care, Melody instituted a regular and active advertising program spending up to $50 weekly on ads in every area newspaper and advertising circular, as well as the Kenosha County Department of Aging's Senior Newsletter. Recently she began advertising in nearby Racine's papers.

She designs her own ads and starts each with: *Are you caring for a dependent adult?* "At first, I always tried to change the message. I've learned that it's more effective to run the same ad. Although the size and shape may vary, now the message remains the same."

A tidbit she'd like to pass along is the importance of previewing a mock-up of ads *before* they run in the paper. She learned the hard way when her handwritten copy was misinterpreted. A list of activities for participants included the words, "Attend Church," which were translated in the ad as 'A hand Church.' "That doesn't make sense at all, but there it was!" Melody finds it helpful to keep copies of all ads in a special notebook. Advertising deadlines for each newspaper are also prominently noted. "Before I started this system, it was chaos."

A typical work day for this busy lady runs from 6:30 AM to 7:00 PM and, until recently, included weekends. (Now she has trimmed those to one per month.) Her afternoon "off" is reserved for driving the boys to favorite activities, like bowling—Adam is the bowler—and roller skating—Aaron is the skater. (A speed-skating champion, his trophies line the shelves in Melody's office.) Early morning regional meets find the entire family on the road before 3:00 AM; upon returning home, Melody reports to work .

"Home" is an apartment upstairs from the day care center. Moving from a home in the country with a large yard to an apartment was a major adjustment for the boys. However, they have learned there are also some advantages, like the fact that Mom is on the premises if they need her. They also enjoy their mom's senior charges and make it a habit to pop in—just to keep in touch. "The patients consider the boys a big part of the program."

Another favorite with the patients is the family dog, a 9-year-old Irish setter called "Dani," who goes from person to person to have her ears scratched, back patted and be told what an extraordinarily fine dog she is.

On the busy afternoon this writer visited Maple Ridge, Melody was shadowed by an elderly gentleman. New to Maple Ridge, he was bewildered and somewhat apprehensive. He followed at Melody's heels as she mingled with patients, distributed cookies and tended to a myriad of administrative duties. When she sat at her desk, he occupied the chair in front of it. She was never less than gracious to him.

It's obvious that Melody enjoys working with older people. "They are interesting. Some are very witty." She claims her greatest reward is witnessing the progress participants in the program make, and cites a case in point. "We had a very depressed woman who was confined to a wheelchair when she first started coming here. Then, as she started going around to visit with the other patients, she transferred to a walker. She began making lots of new friends, came out of her depression, and now doesn't even use a walker."

Just before I left Maple Ridge that afternoon, a lady in a wheelchair called me to her side. She confided that once she was a nurse; now she has Parkinson's disease. Pointing to Melody, she said, "I've never known such a warm and loving person. You know, if it weren't for her. . . I'd be in a nursing home."

"You need to stick to what you believe. You can't give up when the door slams in your face. Don't be afraid to ask questions—keep asking until you understand; otherwise, you may be operating under false pretenses and you'll be doing yourself a disservice. Respect the people you work with and work beside them."

Kay Martyniak
The Gingham Dog

The Gingham Dog isn't the result of a lifelong love affair with the furry creatures. According to Kay Martyniak, her sister was the one who liked dogs. "I didn't pay much attention to them myself."

When "Sherlock," a sheepdog, entered the Martyniak's lives in 1968, he changed all that. Kay recalls that they immediately ran out of space. And, because the city of Chicago wasn't the best environment for an immense and playful puppy, the young couple decided to move to the country. To them, Kenosha, Wisconsin—just on the other side of the Illinois border and with a population of under 70,000—was country.

she also willingly demonstrated her techniques and in the process ended up grooming many a dog. "Pretty soon half my free time was spent showing dogs and the other half, grooming them."

When she began investing in the basic dog grooming equipment—clippers, blades, brushes and combs, a special dryer—her husband Jerry suggested that, as long as she was going that far she might as well open her own grooming shop. Kay was reluctant. "I don't like to make quick decisions because once I make one, I carry through. I didn't think I was aggressive enough to take that first step."

Jerry felt no such compunctions and when he began looking at potential locations for a shop, Kay admitted that there were compelling reasons to move from home base. For one thing, their neighborhood was not zoned for operating a separate shop. And Kay was finding that using the family's sinks and bathtub for bathing dogs wasn't an ideal situation. More importantly, she sensed that people treat a home-based business as if it's not a *real* business. "Because it wasn't a professional setting with regular hours, people assumed they could just drop their dogs off at any time."

The determined Jerry located a perfect spot with reasonable rent on one of Kenosha's main streets. He did everything that needed to be done to the building, except for upgrading the wiring, while Kay secured necessary permits and tax forms. She also thought of a name—The Gingham Dog, borrowed from Eugene Field's poem, *A Gingham Dog and Calico Cat.*

Kay's first advertising campaign consisted of dispensing flyers to "anybody and everybody" as well as placing flyers on windshields of cars and on every bulletin board she saw. Three dogs arrived on opening day, all belonging to friends who kidded, "We want to keep you from starving."

Kay describes the next two months as mostly waiting for the phone to ring. Then came Thanksgiving and a "rush" that lasted through Christmas. Then followed January and February when Kay worried a lot. "The dog grooming business is very seasonal. Things are busiest when people have their dogs dressed up for the Holidays and when they have their carpets cleaned in the spring. We have a big influx of long-haired dogs on the first warm day. Then people want them done yesterday."

It's a mistaken notion that when it's cold a dog's hair doesn't need to be cut. "People don't realize that it's like sitting around in the house all winter with your coat on."

Some dogs come in once a year whether they need it or not. At that point, Kay says, a dog is usually so badly matted she's forced to "peel it—just like a banana"—because the pulling necessary to brush or comb it out would be too much for the dog to tolerate. "Short is better than matted. If the owner is upset, I tell them, 'It will grow back. I'll guarantee it in writing.'"

Kay says that negligence in grooming can be expensive for both owners and groomers. Neglected dogs often develop skin problems and require medicated baths. Like all business people, groomers charge according to the amount of time a particular job takes. Dirty and matted coats also take a heavy toll on grooming equipment. "Coats which are in bad shape can dull up to three blades."

During flea season, which begins in May and ends with the hard frost, Kay is busy giving special flea baths and dips. While flea collars serve as a preventative, they aren't effective once a dog has acquired fleas. "If collars contained chemicals powerful enough to really do the job, the dog would get sick."

As part of her services, Kay removes hair from the dog's ears, checks the anal glands and cuts nails. The finishing touch is a perky ribbon in the colors of the season; orange for Halloween, red and green for Christmas, and red, white and blue for July 4th. On one occasion, lavender was used to match a bride's bouquet. While small dogs look cute with ribbons in their hair, owners of large dogs usually prefer having them attached to the collar. "Teenage boys refuse to have a bow on their dogs."

Ideally, Kay says, a puppy's first grooming should be scheduled before it really needs a hair cut. "That way, we can play with the dog and he learns not to dread going to the groomer. If dogs have a bad experience, they are nervous the next time they come."

Kay's policy is not to accept Pit Bulls. She tried once and was forced to send the dog home an hour later—untouched. German Shepherds also can present problems. "They don't like strangers." Although Kay includes a number of well-behaved Shepherds among her regulars, she's reluctant to accept more, especially if she doesn't know the owners. If she acquiesces and a dog proves difficult to handle, she'll call to inform the owners she's unable to groom it. "I'm paid to groom—not do battle." In such cases, she suggests taking the dog to a groomer affiliated with a veterinarian who can tranquilize it. Because tranquilizers can cause problems for dogs with bad hearts, Kay doesn't use them. In most cases, a stern word is sufficient to settle down a fidgety dog.

The Gingham Dog handles an average of 10-12 dogs a day, though there are fewer on Saturdays when the shop closes early. To assist her, Kay has an almost full-time helper who has been with her for three years. Kay notes that it's hard to find help because the work is seasonal and the burn-out rate is high. Fortunately, the Martyniak offspring, Warren (although he claims he doesn't care for dogs that much), Shawn, and Erin, have become proficient in bathing and drying dogs.

After the last dog leaves, Kay cleans up and washes the floors. She also does all the bookwork herself; however, she has an accountant to handle the taxes. Additionally, she wears the advertising manager's hat.

As part of her advertising program, Kay sends out quarterly "Groom-A-Grams" containing dog-related tidbits; i.e., how to do the Heimlich Maneuver on a choking dog, how a "zig-zag" haircut can make an overweight dog look thinner, and a special section on "groomer humor." Kay addresses the newsletters directly to the dogs. "People seem to get a kick out of mail coming to their dogs."

Occasional ads are placed in free advertising circulars. "They seem to work the best for me and they aren't too expensive. For those just starting out in the business who can only afford to put their money in one place, I suggest the *Yellow Pages*."

The Gingham Dog moved when parking was prohibited on the street. Kay decided on a downtown location because parking was good, rent was reasonable, and the high ceilings and breezes off the nearby lake provided the desired ventilation.

An added attraction has been a life-sized penguin painted in the entrance way. Snazzily outfitted in a tuxedo, the penguin is a leftover from the previous tenant, a men's formalwear store. When customers lamented that "Mr. Penguin" would have to go, Kay hired a local artist to add a sheepdog on a leash to the scene. "Now everyone's happy."

With the new shop, Kay gained not only additional room in which to work, but also twice as much space for pet supplies. The Gingham Dog carries pet supplies, a full line of Science Diet dog foods, and a wide assortment of boutique items. One of Kay's future goals is to build up the retail end of her business. "There's lots of potential because people are becoming more interested in health care for their dogs. They are also more conscious of their dog's appearance. They want them to look nice."

In order to keep apprised of new products, styles, and changes in grooming techniques, Kay attends trade shows and semi-annual seminars. "You learn ways to improve your image. It's also an opportunity to do some networking, which is very important."

She also belongs to the National Dog Groomers Association, the Wisconsin State Dog Groomers Association, and an informal group of local groomers. Kay points out that there are only two male dog groomers in the community; the rest are women. "The main reason women are attracted to dog grooming as a profession is that it works well as a part-time job. You don't have to work when you don't want to work."

Like all moms with outside jobs, Kay juggles her shop with her work at home. She laughs at how difficult it can be to get dinner on the table. "Thank goodness, I have a microwave and we do lots of grilling in the summer. Somehow, things always get done."

In her leisure time, Kay enjoys needlework, especially counted cross stitch. "Someday I'd like to make a quilt." And, of course, with four sheep dogs and three Shih Tzus (small Japanese dogs), there are always dog shows . . . . Since Sherlock, the Martyniaks have had nearly 30 sheepdogs. Obviously, somewhere along the way Kay changed her mind about dogs.

"Dogs are nice; they're like people in many ways. In fact, they're better than people. You can play with them—it's fun. Some are very sociable, while others growl at each other. Some keep busy trying to dig holes in their cages; others cry because they don't like their moms to leave them.

"It's a good feeling to take scruffy dogs and make them look special. You can tell they're proud of their spruced-up appearance. They even begin to prance."

"You need to care about dogs and enjoy them. You need patience—taking the time to pet and play with the dogs can make a crucial difference. Anyone can clip a dog, but it takes special training and lots of practice to develop scissoring and styling talents.

"Getting bitten is a fact of life in the grooming profession. I've had stitches and stitches and stitches. You do everything you can to prevent it, but it can happen when you least expect it.

"It's physically hard work—you're on your feet, lifting heavy dogs and sometimes fighting with dogs. If you're not careful, you can burn out. The rate is five years in this business."

Marilyn McClure
Mrs. Mac's Swim School

The first thing you notice is the laugh. It starts someplace in the tip of her toes, bubbles up and explodes: husky, mischievous, a bit rowdy. It's hardly the kind of laugh you'd expect from a woman who's barely 5' tall. But then, there's not much commonplace about Mrs. Mac or her swim school.

The 1300-square-foot addition to the McClure home which houses the pool is, well, homey. No chilly, slick tile floors and institutional environment here. Opting for paneled walls and carpeted floors, Marilyn tried to correct all the mistakes she'd found in pool areas over the years. To carpet was one of her first decisions. "Floors around a pool are always too slippery. Carpeting is also a lot easier to clean."

Another homey touch is the dog napping alongside the pool (he leaves during classes). "Dagwood," who belongs to son Doug, is referred to by Marilyn as her "Granddog." She reports Dagwood has developed an appetite for pool toys, and thus far has snacked on a boat, two helicopters, and six yellow ducks.

When I accepted an invitation to observe the women's water exercise class in action, I expected bathing-capped, serious-faced women performing drills and calisthenics in the water. Bathing caps? No. Eyeglasses and chunky earrings, yes. Class begins, not with the shrill whistles recalled from my swimming class days, but with the shout, "All right ballerinas, let's go." Serious? Hardly— these women are having a ball. Drills and calisthenics? Try the Hokey Pokey, the "Texas Cowgirl" (everybody bounces up and down as if astride an imaginary horse), and Figure Eights, which accord-ing to Marilyn look more like sixes this night. Before each new exercise, someone in the group wants to know, "What part did you say this builds?"

There are amiable grumbles. "The water seems colder this week." Marilyn nods her head, saying, "I had an ice water delivery this morning because I knew you were coming. I also had a new thermometer put in because you guys complain about the tempera-ture all the time." Then she grins and adds, "It's a rectal thermome-ter."

If being in water is fun for women in the exercise group, it's serious business for the next class I visit. Very. They're here because they're terrified of water. Marilyn reassures a small, visibly tense woman who is steeling herself to duck into the water. "Don't think too hard—it messes you up." The woman shakily submerges. Her head pops up almost immediately. By turns, she is panicky, then embarrassed.

Marilyn tells her, "Don't worry, that's a reflex. We have a tendency to put our heads up first because that's what we do on land. The trouble is when you lift your head too soon when you're in the water, you start to seesaw. You won't lose your balance if you keep your head down, pull your knees up under your stomach, then pick your head up. Should we try it?" With a final assurance that Marilyn will remain nearby, the woman solemnly takes the plunge. This time she does it right. Marilyn whoops with delight.

A few feet away, two middle-aged women cavort in the water. One turns a lopsided somersault. Marilyn calls out, "Next month it's Holiday Inn for you and then we'll go on tour." She points out that only a few months ago this twosome was also fearful of water. "About 80% of my adult students are so scared of water they can hardly get into it."

Afterwards, the women tell me they came to Mrs. Mac because of her reputation for giving students lots of individual attention. They like having their teacher right in the water, not on the deck with a whistle in her mouth. "There's no chiding or threats if you can't cut the mustard." One of Marilyn's maxims is: "Swimming shouldn't hurt."

Mrs. Mac's is a favorite place for Kenoshans to introduce their tiny tykes to swimming. According to Marilyn, it's easier teaching infants and very young children to swim than their older counterparts. "Older kids make up their minds in advance that they don't want to be here. They make up excuses like, 'I can't swim today—I have a headache.' I've even had a few threaten to let the water out of the pool. In the end, they begin to enjoy it."

Marilyn herself was introduced to swimming at the age of six when she spent two months at a summer camp. She enjoyed it so much she returned for the next seven summers. Eventually, she began teaching the younger campers how to swim. As a high school student she joined the synchronized swim team. "I liked the grace and beauty of synchronized swimming. Competitive swimming didn't appeal to me because I'm not a competitive person."

Just seventeen when she graduated from high school, Marilyn enrolled at the University of Illinois to pursue a major in Physical Education. Her plans changed the day she stopped at a drugstore for a Coke and met John McClure, a "gorgeous fella." Three months later, she became his bride.

Several moves (John was in the Air Force) and three children later, Marilyn found herself once again in the role of swimming teacher, this time for a large institution. She resigned when she became disenchanted with the methods of instruction employed there. "Many of my fearful students are the direct result of those types of teaching methods."

When she read about a woman who started a swim school in her home, she thought, "Why not?" John gave the project his blessing, but made it perfectly clear it was *her* project. Few friends were encouraging. "People told us we were both nuts. It was like it was the doomsday machine."

When she called the local zoning authorities she learned there was no precedent. "The closest thing to a swim school on the books was a turkish bath." She was advised that the pool would have to be enclosed and attached to the main dwelling. In addition to safety and rescue equipment, special electrical outlets were required, as was a telephone for the pool area. "I decided to build over code and have more safety features than the city called for."

Additionally, she was to inform neighbors of her plans to build an extensive addition to the house, even though from the outside, it isn't possible to tell there's a pool on the premises. She would also have to advise them regarding the amount of traffic her business would be likely to bring into the neighborhood. "I told everyone that if they ever had any problems to come to me." Thus far, there haven't been any complaints.

When John told her the swim school was her project, he meant it. As general contractor for the project, Marilyn did it all—from deciding who would install the pool, to buying a heater, filters, etc., to applying for a loan. She recalls that it took three weeks to find a local institution willing to talk to her. "I went right down the list in the phone book. I'm stubborn and I was determined to find someone." Her persistence paid off and in due time there was a 16' x 32' mud hole in the backyard. That's when the enormity of the project hit her. "I'd look at it and say, 'Go away. Disappear.' "

Mrs. Mac's Swim School opened its doors on December 14, 1981. Sole advertising was a week of classifieds in the local paper. "That's all I could afford." Despite her worries that no one would come, enough students enrolled to form a class, which burgeoned after a feature story in the local newspaper. She no longer recalls the numbers or other details of that first class. "Everything was a blur."

She knew Mrs. Mac's was a success when repeat business came for the second session of classes. Once a family enrolls a member, she eventually gets them all. She is especially proud of the fact that, when families move to other parts of the country, they take great pains to schedule lessons for their up-and-coming swimmers to coincide with vacation periods when the family returns to visit Kenosha.

Mrs. Mac's programs consist of ten weeks of swimming lessons. People register for classes in advance. A deposit isn't necessary; the fee is payable at the first session. "People are very good. I've never been burned." Make-up lessons are available if it's necessary for a student to miss a class. "People appreciate that because in most situations that class would be lost."

Although she spends nine hours a day, four days a week in the water, Marilyn has never had a sick day. "I talk to my body and keep telling it 'You do not have anything wrong.' " With a twinkle in her eyes, she suggests that her good health can be credited to her diet: malted milk balls, Oreo cookies, and Twinkies. Despite this, she remains trim enough to purchase the ten bathing suits she wears out yearly at a children's clothing store. According to Marilyn, she doesn't burn up calories swimming. "I actually don't do that much. Swimming isn't taught by demonstrating. People learn through doing."

In addition to her swim teacher role, Marilyn is also the pool cleaner, water tester, telephone receptionist and bookkeeper. Her "office" space is shared with John, who also owns a business, JMC Packaging. Each gets half the kitchen table. Her side consists of a jumbo straw basket heaping with papers.

When not busy with Mrs. Mac duties, Marilyn says her family lets her have the car on Saturday mornings for two hours so she can grocery shop. "I'm also the maid—I do toilets." She is quick to point out that if everything doesn't get done, no one fusses.

The McClure's three good-looking sons, Russell, Douglas, and Bradley, were already in high school when Marilyn started her swim school. "I could trust them. They had good heads on their shoulders." She went on to say her family has always appreciated the fact that she's accessible to them whenever needed.

The down side to her line of work is "looking like a prune all the time. You have to shave your legs a lot." Then too, she has this little problem: People constantly approach her in restaurants and at the grocery store with, "Hi there, I almost didn't recognize you with your clothes on."

"On this job, I get to laugh all day. You wouldn't believe the things that are said around this pool! It's great seeing results right before your eyes and then there's the special satisfaction of having built a business—that's the American Dream."

"You have to have faith. If you don't take a chance on anything, you'll have nothing. With the support of those closest to you, you'll have the strength to do anything."

Portrait by George Pollard

Diane Mikic
Monya's Beauty Salon

Often referred to as "Kenosha's Auntie Mame," Diane Mikic is vivacious, entertaining, audacious, witty, a pistol, one-of-a-kind. Like the celebrated Mame, Diane embraces a "life is a banquet" philosophy. Also like Mame, she's adept at coining slogans. While others claim they need a change, Diane needs "more juice—more adrenaline" and then she takes the appropriate action.

Another favorite motto is: "Learn how to do it." Add to that, "the earlier the better." Diane's lived accordingly. Billed as "the little girl with the big voice," she was singing professionally at age 13.

At 18, she met an attractive man from Germany, who was in the United States to promote soccer. Diane married him, and (although the marriage didn't last) gave birth to a son, Mark, who became one of the enduring joys of her life. While married, she added German to the list of languages she speaks fluently (she also speaks Polish, Slo-vak, Czech, and Croatian).

That was in the early sixties. Although the abiding rule at that time was for pregnant women to automatically retire from the workplace at the four-month point, Diane worked up until one week before Mark was born. Shortly afterwards, baby and diaper bag accompanied her to the dental office where she worked. "It took three bus transfers to get us there." This was a pattern that continued for the next four years. While his mom worked, young Mark gazed in wonder at the exotic fish cavorting in the huge aquarium which dominated the waiting room. Later, as a toddler and then pre-schooler, he occupied himself with crayons, books, and a lively interest in all who passed through the office doors.

Diane states her employer encouraged the unique child care arrangement. Not only did he love children and have nine of his own, he also specialized in children's dentistry. She says, "I hope some day all businesses will realize that people work better with their children around and will begin to provide space for child care. That way people could have lunch with their children and drop by during the day. They wouldn't be distracted worrying about them." She adds, "It would be worth the expense involved. After all, the child is our best investment."

When Mark proudly marched off to kindergarten, Diane decided it was time for (what else?) more juice—more adrenaline, and so she entered beauty school. She had grown up in the beauty business. Her mother, Monya Pinno, owned and operated a beauty salon which adjoined the family home. Diane, who recalls making pin curls as a six-year-old, exhibited her mother's talent for styling hair.

A dedicated and energetic student, she captured top honors at City College South (Milwaukee) and, in her own words, was promoted from "Queen of the Mop" to "Queen of the Hop" when she was selected as queen from among nine accredited beauty schools. (The award was based on classwork, grades and performance in a production of the student's choosing. Diane wowed them in her version of *The Unsinkable Molly Brown*.)

After acquiring her Manager's License, Diane went on to become a Manager for one of the Regis beauty salons in the Milwaukee area. She was also a sales representative for Eva Gabor's and Jerome Alexander's line of wigs, and says she found Gabor, whom she met a number of occasions, to be a nice, as well as lovely, boss who paid a good salary.

Diane particularly recalls the time she was summoned to a show at the last moment to substitute for another wig stylist. She was in the pool when the call came and there wasn't time to dry her hair (it was nearly down to her waist at the time)—so she tried to camouflage it. Gabor quickly spotted the huge, bright yellow hat atop Diane's head—it was attracting more attention than the wigs on display. Making a beeline through the crowd, she directed Diane: "Take off that hat, my darling," and with that, proceeded to remove the offending hat. Nonplussed, Diane recaptured the hat, popped it back on her head and announced, "Not until you find me a wig to cover this wet hair, my darling." Gabor promptly and graciously complied. Ever afterwards when the twosome crossed paths, the actress laughingly brought up the subject of "that hat."

Diane's sales representative days ended when her mother, after 27 years in the hairdressing business, decided to retire and sell Monya's Beauty Salon. She gave Diane first chance to buy it. Diane says it took less than a week to decide. "I was too sentimental about that little shop to allow it to go into someone else's hands."

Another compelling reason for Diane's decision to buy the business was the opportunity to operate a business at home. "It was a wonderful way to raise my son. I could make money and watch over him at the same time. It's hard to find proper care for a child. If the mother feels guilty about going to work, that guilt is passed on to the child."

Although Monya's has been given several facelifts and new operators are on the scene, a significant number of the original patrons still come for weekly washes and sets. Some retain their original hairstyles. Diane says the greatest compliment she receives from these long-time patrons is: "Diane, you've got it!" Translated: "It looks as though Monya herself did my hair!"

Describing the differences between her mother's business and her own, Diane says, "The sixties were a glamour era. The women wore long gowns and came in frequently for updo's. Now everything's more casual." Bypassing time-consuming elaborate hairstyles, today's women think "tinting, frosting, highlighting or voluminization"—a technique where operators wax extensions to existing hair—when they want to create a special look.

Not surprisingly, hair coloring is one of Monya's specialties. "There are wonderful products available now which are so gentle on the hair." According to Diane, today's operators are more educated and more knowledgeable about the texture and chemistry of hair, because hairdressing is more technical now. She adds that patrons are also more informed about their hair.

Other differences between Monya's then and now is that today many men come in regularly—something that was virtually unheard of 20 years ago—and wigs are not as commonplace as they were in the late 60's and early 70's. Then it appeared that every woman who could afford a wig owned at least one. Now, Diane says, most women prefer to wear their hair in "wash and wear" styles. "They don't feel a need for wigs. " However, she styles wigs frequently for people who have lost their hair as the result of chemotherapy treatments and says it's rewarding to make them look good.

At this writing, waves and bobs are making a comeback. "There's more softness now. More glitz." Owner of one of the glitziest bouffants in town, Diane chuckles, "In New York, my kind of hair is in." She adds, "Come a new season, there'll be another look." From beehives to French twists to shags to wedges to Mohawks to punk, Diane has done it all. "Even if I wouldn't wear most of them with my fur coat, it's fun. That's what hairdressing should be."

Diane prides herself on the fact that all the equipment in her shop is American-made. Although overhead dryers and freeflow bowls are now being manufactured overseas, she's not tempted to invest in them. "I know Europeans and Japanese won't be paying my social security or pension. Americans will be—so it's everything American for me."

Something else Diane feels strongly about is the disservice beauticians do to their profession when they perform beauty services from their homes. "Because of the low overhead involved, home operators can undercut beauty salons. Those who patronize them may pay a bit less; however, they are also at greater risk. When these home operators don't report their income, they are cheating the IRS. They should be proud of the license they earned and abide by it."

As her business grew, so did son Mark, whom she describes as being raised on lots of laughter, music and kissing. Mark, who is a published writer and will soon receive his Doctorate in Counseling Psychology, was the one who introduced Diane to her second husband, Frank Mikic, a Senior Project Engineer at Snap-on Tools. It was Frank who led her into COSMETECH, an exciting second business.

Shortly after their marriage in 1975, Diane learned her husband's hobby was inventing things. It was a time-consuming hobby and Diane admits at first she felt left out. "Then I decided if you can't fight it, join it, so I asked him to invent something I could relate to — something to do with the beauty business."

During meetings of the Kenosha Hair Stylists Association, Diane had become acquainted with Frank Fani, owner and operator of the Flair Styling Studio in Kenosha, and learned that Fani was not only very technically inclined and keenly interested in new product design, but also was, like her husband Frank, an inventor. She arranged for the two to meet and reports that, after only a few cups of coffee, they had a unique-looking comb down on a paper napkin. Thus, the birth of the "Shortcut," an ingenious comb/hair-cutting guide that reduces the time for a precision hair cut from 20 minutes to only five or ten. The Shortcut is also excellent for blow drying and finish work.

A prototype of the comb was quickly developed. Son Mark, who is producer and director of *Joy Farm*, an award-winning cable comedy/music program which is aired nationally, then produced a video of the Shortcut in action using live models. After creating a striking display booth, the two Franks were off to a trade show in New York accompanied by Diane and Fani's wife, Janet.

That was only the beginning. From the phenomenal response, it looks as though the Shortcut and COSMETECH will be a "shared adventure" in the Mikic's lives for a long time to come.

"Having a good personality is extremely important to success in this business. You owe it to your customer to be at your best. You're always on stage and the show must always go on no matter what. Of course, you should have some natural ability with hair.

"Be ready to work hard. There's no such thing as an eight-hour day. Take into consideration that you'll be standing in one place most of the day. If you don't have a strong back and legs, you won't be able to take it. Also, there are lots of chemicals involved, so you need to be aware in case you have any allergies. Attend as many classes and seminars in salon training as possible.

"Believe in yourself. Take a self-inventory once in a while; look back at your life and be honest in that inventory. Hire people in the areas where you're deficient; then trust and believe in those you hire. Work as a family. The key to success isn't only money— but peace of mind, knowing you have made this a better place to live in. Maybe even spread some joy."

Marlene Mura
Barbie Bazaar

She's a captivating public speaker who can make her audience howl with laughter one moment and reach for their hankies the next. She's an outspoken advocate for women's rights, dating back to her grammar school days when she questioned why girls weren't allowed to become crossing guards. She's prominent on Kenosha, Wisconsin's civic and political scene. She's a writer. She sells insurance—her specialty is coverage for small businesses. And finally, she's a long-time volunteer for the Girl Scouts. So when Marlene Mura revealed she was launching a magazine, most of her friends took for granted it would be an offshoot of one of these activities.

If the truth be known, when they learned Marlene was writing and producing a magazine about Barbie (that's right, Barbie—as in "doll"), they chortled with disbelief. Even Marlene admits she can hardly believe it. She then goes on to point out that Barbie represents more than just a doll with a curvaceous figure and fabulous wardrobe. "She plays a multi-dimensional role and has had a significant impact on girls in America. Barbie crosses racial as well as international boundaries—that's why we've named her the 'Ambassador of Friendship.' "

When Barbie came along to change the face of the doll world forever, Marlene was already busy combining raising babies and going to college. With her husband Richard's encouragement, she attended Carthage College in Kenosha part-time and was graduated in 1970 with a degree in Elementary Education. Although she considered teaching a good experience, she didn't choose to make it her lifetime career. (She really had wanted to enroll in Business Administration, but was told it would be more sensible to take a secretarial course. "Most working women were in traditional supportive roles. There wasn't any concept of career women yet.")

Marlene's accomplishments (in addition to earning a college degree while raising a family—no small feat in itself) are many and varied. She was the youngest president in the history of the St. Catherine's Hospital Auxiliary, as well as the first woman to be appointed to the Hospital's Board of Directors. She's been elected twice to serve as chair of the city's powerful Fire and Police Commission. She has been chairperson for the Mayor's Commission on Human Relations, the Kenosha County Coordinated Planning and Budget Committees, and the Kenosha Women's Network's Political and Economic Committee. She has been a member of the Kenosha County Comprehensive Board; a delegate for Kenosha to the Governor's Conference on Small Business; the Vice President of the United Way fundraising campaign; and a participant in Focus 2000, a goal-setting program for the city of Kenosha, targeted toward the year 2000.

Keenly interested in politics, too, Marlene ran for County Board Supervisor in 1982 and won the primary—but lost the general election. In 1984 she made a nearly successful bid for a seat in the Wisconsin State Legislature. Despite the fact that her campaign funds were slight and she had little political clout, she came in second out of ten candidates. She says that she would run for the post again if the opportunity presented itself. "My heart is in the state legislature."

Amidst all these commitments, Marlene managed to find time to become an impressive public speaker, an independent insurance agent, and a dedicated volunteer with the Girl Scouts.

Her Girl Scout activities brought her into contact with Karen Caviale, Kenosha Scout Director and owner of 350 Barbie dolls, at last count. As for Marlene, she vaguely remembers buying her daughters a Barbie or two.

Because both Marlene and Karen are of an entrepreneurial bent, every time they met, their conversations would turn to possible business ventures they might embark upon together. Marlene says that Barbie's name kept popping up in these conversations. "I'd always laugh. I couldn't believe people would pay big dollars—sometimes it runs in the thousands—for a 12-and-a-half-inch doll!" She kept laughing until one day the idea of adult fascination with Barbie finally took hold.

The twosome met evenings and weekends to talk "Barbie talk." They put together a survey querying samplings of Barbie Club members (there are 500,000 of them throughout the United States and abroad.) "We wanted to determine the level of interest in a magazine for adult Barbie collectors. The response was unbelievable." They discovered that Barbie fans were hungry for anything "Barbie" they could get their hands on. With Barbie's 30th anniversary just around the corner in 1989, the market was ripe for a Barbie magazine.

After conversations with scores of people in the publishing field, the two women decided it was time to take the plunge. Ten months after they had their first serious Barbie conversation, Marlene and Karen purchased a Mac II computer, a DEST PC Scan 1000 Apple laser printer, an optical scanner, and an assortment of desktop publishing software programs, including Quark Express and Writer II for inputting text, Adobe Illustrator for page layout, and Microsoft Works for spreadsheets. "At that point, we knew we were in really deep." *Barbie Bazaar* was on its way.

A major goal would be publishing the first adult collector's magazine about Barbie, the world's most famous doll. Additionally, they also saw *Barbie Bazaar* as a vehicle for artists, illustrators, and writers aspiring to be published. Collectors would also be invited to share their stories, ideas, and viewpoints. Everyone would be given credit for their contributions. "We feel that if we can make a little success for someone else, that's good. We want others to be part of this adventure."

The magazine features tidbits which beguile even those who don't claim to be Barbie fans. For example, the Sanlorel Barbie Doll Collector's Club of Sandusky, Ohio, shared details of their Valentine's Day extravaganza. Picture a 36" table seating 20 Barbies and their macho dates—no Kens were allowed. In a setting all dec-orated with hearts, including tiny paper plates, napkins, and plastic glasses, the guests exchanged wee valentines.

Monthly columns include "Meet a Collector" department, "Dazzling Designs," "News from Japan Barbie," and words of wis-dom from Dr. Dan, the Barbie Doctor.

Marlene recalls how people scoffed before they saw the pre-miere issue. But—thanks to award-winning professional photogra-pher James P. Dowling (Milwaukee), whose weeks of planning and endless hours of shooting go into each of the dozen or so full-color spreads in each magazine—she now says of the high-gloss monthly, "People didn't expect to see a classy, sophisticated magazine. We knew it was going to be good, but not *that* good!"

Experts in the field state that originating a new magazine takes a minimum of $500,000. Marlene agrees that's a realistic esti-mate. To cut costs, she and Karen do virtually all of the work themselves instead of hiring employees.

Karen is the computer expert who designs *Barbie Bazaar's* eye-catching layouts. She also writes many of the articles. As sub-scription director, Marlene, who barely had a nodding acquaintance with computers, took a "crash course" in order to handle the spread-sheet program for subscriptions. Additionally, she wears the hats of contributing editor, and business office manager. Public relations and promotions are joint endeavors. (Both also continue to work at their regular jobs, Marlene as an insurance consultant and Karen as director of Kenosha's Girl Scout Office.)

Family members pitch in by checking every magazine for correct color reproduction, counting magazines in every case for ac-curate numbers, sticking on address labels, and encasing the maga-zines in plastic bags for mailing, all tasks which Marlene lists as the "least favorite" aspects of her business. Karen's mother (also an avid Barbie collector) donated her basement recreation room as head-quarters for Murat-Caviale Communications, Inc.

Marlene's husband Richard constructed the circular stage

81

shown on the cover of the September issue featuring 1967's Black Francie, when she was crowned "Miss Teenage Beauty." He also invented a special sealing machine for the mailing bags.

Like other successful women, Marlene realizes the value of her family's constant support for her many endeavors. "We're a tight family." She says of her husband, "I'm fortunate because he wants my success." The Muras are proud of their three children: Michelle, a University of Wisconsin-LaCrosse graduate who works for Hartford Insurance; Renee, a student at the University of Wisconsin-Milwaukee; and John, a senior at Mary D. Bradford High School.

This past year has included periods of both great exhilaration and despair. Marlene and Karen would survive one crisis, only to face another. "We were really green. If we had known at the beginning what the project entailed, we probably wouldn't have begun."

Perhaps their biggest mistake was deciding to publish a monthly magazine. "It's impractical. Publishing monthly takes an incredible amount of time and energy. At this point, we are still a small operation and do everything ourselves. We need more time to devote to promotion and other aspects of the business." Thus the decision to eventually become a bi-monthly magazine.

If at times they feel overwhelmed (there's hardly a breath between issues), the two women say they also experience enormous satisfactions. Such as going to a Barbie convention and being treated like celebrities, obtaining new advertising accounts, and watching the numbers of subscribers climb toward their goal of 20,000—that's the magic number when they feel they'll be able to devote themselves full-time to their business.

"We're proud of *Barbie Bazaar*. We did what we said we would do. It's been a great and thrilling adventure."

To receive sample copy of "Barbie Bazaar," send $4.95 to:

Murat Caviale Communications, Inc.
2526-80th Place
Kenosha, WI 53140

"Starting a business takes time, commitment and financial resources. If you enjoy it and have fun, it makes the commitment easier. Don't become too greedy for success. If you share something, you'll get something back. Leadership can afford to be generous."

"Always try to be a friend. Don't put down the very women who have worked for years to open the door of opportunity for you. No person is successful because of only herself or himself. If you feel defeated, find someone you can help—someone who needs you more than YOU need you."

Dorothy Patel
Crown Host Inn

If you ask Dorothy Patel why she decided to go into the motel business, she'll tell you she married into it. Soft-spoken, with a trace of a Texas drawl, Dorothy explains her original plan was to become a band director. A music major at Angelo State University (San Angelo, Texas) and pressed for money, she decided to take a part-time job as a waitress. When she walked into the Las Brisas Motor Inn, she had no idea that she was about to change her entire life.

Manny Patel managed the restaurant in addition to the ad-joining motel. Before long he and Dorothy began dating. By the time he moved to Arkansas to manage a larger motel, the relationship had blossomed, and continued long distance. Dorothy, who changed her course of studies from Music to Psychology, was only one class short of graduation when they decided to get married; she left college and joined him to manage the motel in Arkansas.

Dorothy smiles as she recalls that first Ma-Pa operation. "We lived there and did everything ourselves. Manny was the night desk clerk and sometimes had to sleep in his clothes."

Impressed by the way the Patels managed to bring the little motel through some tough times, the mortgage holder approached the Patels to join him as partners for a Wisconsin motel that was on the market. Thus, Dorothy found herself the co-owner of an 85-room motel in Kenosha, Wisconsin.

After the little Ma-Pa operation, this was big time. A full-service motel, the facility contains a restaurant, lounge, and swimming pool, in addition to its 85 bedrooms. There are also several large rooms available for banquets, parties, and meetings.

Another major change is overseeing a large staff. The Patels employ 15 workers including three full-time desk clerks, a housekeeper who supervises the laundry and seven room attendants, a night auditor, someone to handle accounts receivable, and a combination porter-janitor-gofer. "We're lucky to have a wonderful staff. Some have been here a long time. A few have gone on to bigger and better things. It's always hard to replace someone in this business because it's hard work and the pay is low."

The Patels immediately faced a major challenge: establishing the motel's new identity as the Crown Host Inn. Although its official name had been the Midway Motor Lodge, everyone called it "Nino's," which was the name of the popular adjoining restaurant. When Nino's went out of business, everyone assumed the motel was also closed. "One of the first things we did was change the name to Crown Host Inn and erect a huge sign." Ruefully, she adds, " Some people still refer to it as Nino's."

The Patels soon discovered that while pools are popular with visitors, they also entail a great deal of work. "There are about a hundred things that can go wrong." Then too, state and city health departments have set a multitude of rules and regulations governing pools. Not only that, they send someone once a month to check things out. A steep rise in insurance rates prompted them to briefly consider covering the pool with a deck and turning it into a game room. "Finally, we found insurance we could afford."

Although she and Manny work together smoothly most of the time, Dorothy states, "There are times when we yell at each other, mostly because we have different ideas." On the plus side, the differences in their personalities simplify scheduling work hours. Manny is an early bird who prefers to work during the day, while Dorothy confesses she likes to sleep late. "I don't mind working second shift."

As to weekly hours, Dorothy says it would be hard to estimate how many she works. "I'm in and out all the time." Hours are kept flexible to accommodate household duties, young daughter Crystal's activities, and Dorothy's outside interests, such as serving on the Hotel/Motel Advisory Committee for Gateway Technical College, on a subcommittee for Kenosha's Convention and Travel Bureau, and playing clarinet in the Kenosha Symphony.

On days when Crystal isn't in school, she accompanies her mom to work. "She's old enough to have the run of the place and enjoys sitting in the pool. Of course, she's well acquainted with the candy machines in the lobby."

It's this kind of flexibility that Dorothy ranks as one of the chief benefits of being self-employed. "It permits you to set your own schedule, at least within limits. You reap what you sow—the more you put in, the more you get out." She points out, however, that there is a flip side in the motel business. "You get the hours no one else wants. I can automatically plan on working Thanksgiving and Christmas."

While lazy summer days mean slowing down for most people, it's the busiest time of the year for motel owners. From mid-June to Labor Day, vacationers and business travelers fill the rooms. (Her idea of a nightmare is to have a packed motel on a warm Saturday night when the air conditioning suddenly stops working.) During the rest of the year, occupancy is mostly by business travelers.

Surprisingly, she and Manny put in longer, if less harried, hours in the winter. Not only do most of the staff take their vacations during that time, it's an opportunity for the Patels to cut costs by doing much of the extra work themselves. They have found the off-season to be a good time to schedule major projects. "We try to do one a year." Thus far, they have repainted the exterior, repaved the parking lot, recarpeted a major hallway, and installed new window-unit heat pumps, which are combination air conditioner-heating units.

Before the new units were installed, Dorothy says there were certain rooms that couldn't be used during the winter. "The boiler is 20 years old and was installed before people were conscious of energy efficiency. We had to supplement it with individual space heaters. Now we don't have to use the boiler anymore."

If it's hard work, running a motel can also be rewarding. "You meet different people every day. There are new situations every day, so you're never bored."

Dorothy admits the motel business can be discouraging at times. "The worst thing is having people trash their rooms. Crown Host doesn't own a T.V. set without at least one burn on it." T.V. controls must be hidden to prevent people from playing with them. "They try to get around that by ripping the covers off." Of course, there are always vanishing towels and glasses. "People think no one will notice, but we always know when they take things or let an extra person in. You develop an instinct."

Dorothy went on to tell about the time several travelers left a suitcase behind in the parking lot. "We opened the suitcase looking for identification and found a few clothes, along with our towels, glasses, and toilet paper, plus glasses from the restaurant." (She chuckles). "That suitcase never did get claimed."

"Fortunately," she says, "most people are nice. They are courteous and tell us how much they liked the accommodations. But, you're always going to find a few—the kind who stay the whole night and then try to get a refund at check-out time because they claim their room was a dump." (Standard motel policy is: *Once you've stayed, there are no refunds.*)

Surprisingly, noise complaints are minimal. "I guess it's because we have things down to a science. We know how to arrange people now, and always place the party animals in a section away from the families and business travelers."

Dorothy's major responsibility is overseeing the front desk where things can get hectic, especially on Friday and Saturday nights. "You have to watch reservations carefully so you don't overbook." She also tends to daily correspondence and the mammoth amount of paperwork a motel business demands. Her job was made easier when daily operating reports were computerized. "It eliminated all the huge binders we had to keep."

They plan their advertising program together. Things like a large ad in the Yellow Pages, a billboard sign at the Kenosha Twin's ball park, and, most recently, a toll-free "800" number for reservations. Dorothy says they have many ideas they'd like to try; however, they found ideas aren't always easy to implement. "I guess marketing is our weak spot."

The Patels always dreamed of opening a second motel some day. "We decided we would locate it near the interstate. That way it could serve as a feeder for the Crown Host, whose location isn't as visible as we'd like it to be."

This spring that dream came true, when the 24-unit Park Ridge Inn opened. Additions are planned for the future. Still another dream was living in a home of their own. This also came true; their new site included a large home, which they are busy remodeling.

There are still dreams to be fulfilled. Dorothy, a 1987 graduate of the University of Wisconsin-Parkside in Kenosha, with a major in Psychology and a minor in Spanish, would like a teaching certificate which would enable her to work with Spanish-speaking people. They also dream of visiting Manny's relatives in Gujerat, India, but will wait until daughter Crystal is older (young children without built-up immunities can become very ill there). Until this visit is possible, they enjoy short jaunts to "Little India" on Devon Street in Chicago.

"You need to be in good health because it's a 24-hour operation. Be prepared to WORK! If you run short-handed, you fill in— even for the housekeeper. You can't be afraid to get your hands and knees dirty, so forget the idea of sitting in an air-conditioned office all day with your own secretary. That doesn't happen except on a T.V. series."

Colleen Perri
Possibilities Publishing

Editor's Note: As requested, I'm including my own story in this second volume of my three part set, "Entrepreneurial Women."

I come from a family that abounds with writers. My great uncle was a newspaper editor; my mother writes poetry; my brother, novels and my daughter, newsletters. At the age of eight, I launched my writing career with an official letter of complaint directed to my mother after she presented me with yet another little brother, despite my strict orders to have a girl. When the next two babies were girls, I decided writing was a good way to change things I didn't like. I've been operating on that principle ever since.

As a high school student, whenever my budget suffered a serious shortfall, I'd enter an essay contest. My winnings ranged from $3 to a glorious $25 savings bond. Later, as the mother of three small children, including a set of twins, I earned pin money writing fillers (mostly helpful household hints and kiddie humor) for newspapers and obscure little magazines.

Determined to become a professional writer, I attended college on a course-at-a-time plan, and was graduated from the University of Wisconsin-Parkside in Kenosha with a degree in Communication—just in time to feel proud at my 25th high school reunion.

My career path was anything but straight. First, I was a writer for a religious organization (my specialty was ... er ... begging letters); then a rental agent for a large apartment complex (writing was largely "your rent is overdue—turn down your stereo—you can't keep that dog" type missives); followed by Activities Director for Kenosha county's senior citizen nutrition program (I was the happy little "Game Lady"); five years as a glorified secretary at the local university (in addition to reporting endless meeting minutes, I had the unique opportunity to write a student employment handbook—by committee); and finally, I served as Executive Director for the local downtown business association. Along with planning district promotions, I produced several monthly newsletters. It wasn't enough. After 12 years of writing for others, I decided it was time to write for myself.

Rather than seek a publisher and tread the well-known rejection slip path, I decided to start my own publishing company. I heard that if I applied for a loan at the bank, I'd have a better chance of being accepted if I said I needed the money for a car or vacation; so I took out a loan at my Church Credit Union to purchase a Macintosh Plus computer, Microsoft word processing and Pagemaker graphics programs.

That was in 1986. Possibilities Publishing's first project: a book focusing on the entrepreneurial women in my hometown of Kenosha, Wisconsin. It was my contention that women in business in our community suffered from extremely low visibility. For example, when I contacted the Chamber of Commerce for a list of women-owned businesses, I was informed that there were not even enough to warrant typing a list. Through my own exhaustive research I learned there are more than 300!

The first six months of *Entrepeneurial Women's* life were the stuff of my dreams. Thanks to a nice article in the local paper and write-ups in *Inside Business* and *Wisconsin Woman* Magazine, and *Sideline Business* Newsletter, sales the first few months were brisk. For the first time in my life, I made more than $1,000 in one week— I was in Heaven!

Encouraged, I immediately threw myself into *Entrepreneurial Women - Book II*. I also initiated "Press on the Desk," a series of newsletters offering resources, ideas and tips for writers and self-publishers, based on my experiences both in self- and desktop publishing. (The issue on "How to Become a Hometown Author" was my bestseller. Apparently there are lots of would-be writers around the country eager to carve their niche by writing about noteworthy people and places in their own communities.)

Immersed in writing, I let things go merrily along until one day it dawned me on that three weeks had passed without a single sale. That turned into four, then five. Suddenly Dan Poynter's words came back to me. Poynter, known as the guru of self-publishers and the author of *The Self-Publishing Manual* (which was my Bible throughout my writing project) states that in order to make a decent living, self-publishers should spend 5% of their time writing and the other 95% marketing. I was doing just the opposite!

I hustled into a marketing program consisting of an ongoing series of classified ads in Mother's Home Business Network's Newsletter plus a display ad in their once a year mailpak. I can't believe the steady flow of orders through those inexpensive classifieds. I love it! Locally, I used a combination of direct mail and classified and display newspaper ads. Direct mail proved to be most effective for me. Of course, the beauty of writing "hometown" books, is being able to pinpoint your audience.

I realize that if I'm going to make it in this business, I need to concentrate my time, energy and money on the marketing area. (For one year, maybe I won't write anything. Groan!)

At times, my life seems like a precarious balancing act between meeting project deadlines, and trying to the pay the bills. The latter has involved offering desktop publishing tutoring sessions, resumé writing services, and teaching seminars on "How to Start a Home-based Business" and "Newsletter Writing," among other topics. I even signed on for a three-week stint as an office temporary when my computer was out of commission. (Without my little Mac, I felt as helpless as if I had lost an arm or leg.)

That owning and running my own business wouldn't be easy didn't come as a surprise. Before I ventured forth into the entrepreneurial waters I spent almost a year researching, including doing a Business Feasibility Study through the Small Business Development Center and meeting with a retired publisher through the Service Corps of Retired Executives (SCORE) program. (All time well spent.) Thus, I was well aware of the fact that it can take years to establish a niche in the marketplace. I keep telling myself, "Wait until next year!"

Right now, I'm at the stage where I put most of my earnings directely back into the business. Major purchases have been a Canon photocopier, a hard disk for the computer, and an Apple Laserwriter printer. In order to buy that marvelous printer, I gave up the luxury of my own wheels. Sometimes, when I stand shivering at the bus stop, I wonder, momentarily, if it was worth it.

Then I recall the days before I became the proud owner of a printer. Little box of disks in hand, I was forced to travel 16 miles to another community where a desktop publisher would run copies of my work on her laser printer. Perhaps this arrangement would have worked for someone less revision-happy. As for me, I'd no sooner get home than I was ready to go straight back with a new batch of corrections in hand. Frustration!

That wasn't my only lesson in learning that skimping on equipment can be costly in the long run. In an attempt to keep costs down, I postponed purchasing a hard disk, thinking I could function adequately with a small external disk drive. Not so. The Pagemaker program I was using was so large it utilized most of the available memory. As a result, there was only room to input a chapter or two and then the inevitable "disk full" message would appear. If I didn't file off immediately the file was lost. It was cumbersome and time-consuming and I said goodbye to more than one file in the process.

In order to buy equipment, there have been other sacrifices in addition to my car—like going without a vacation for three years. And I'm still waiting for a new winter coat and drapes for the front room. Yet, as far as I'm concerned, the sacrifices have been well worth it. I love making all my own decisions, setting my own hours, and, most of all, writing what *I* want to write. To me, these things are infinitely more important than a regular paycheck. (Although that would be nice too.)

I find that working from home suits me perfectly. It takes an extremly self-motivated person to combat the constant temptation to put the business on the back burner—just until after that favorite TV show, little snooze, or phone call. As a workaholic, I have few problems motivating myself to press on, no matter what. In fact, stopping to eat, sleep and relax is harder for me.

However, not all problems common to home-based businesses have been bypassed so easily. I always heard it said that a business tends to take over the home. It's true! My family now lives in a "one bedroom-two office" home—to say nothing of the boxes of books that have spilled over into the family room. I already have my eye on the room in the basement that our college age son will be abandoning in another year. Fortunately, we have the space to spare; otherwise, I don't know what I'd do.

When I was forewarned about the isolation factor and the difficulties it can cause home-based workers, I thought "Not me!" I'm a person who thrives on quiet and solitude. I had no idea how much I would miss working around people. After my first winter working at home, I was so starved for news about the "outside world" that I'd literally pounce on my poor husband when he got home from work.

A partial solution to this dilemma was breaking up the days with outside errands and luncheon appointments. Better yet was taking on a partner, Maureen Reed (who also owns a home-based business), for a special venture. Together, we published *Her Pages*, the first annual directory of Kenosha women's skills, services, and products.

It's been grand having Maureen for a partner: I can bounce ideas off her, share with her those rarefied moments when things go according to plan, and commiserate with her when things go awry. An additional benefit in having a partner is that we can keep each other on target. If one of us is having a down day, the other one gets things going again. We energize each other.

As the owner of a small publishing company, one of my biggest problems has been turning away the onslaught of people seeking a publisher. With a staff of one-and-a-half (my daughter serves as my very part-time secretary), I have more work than I can handle just producing my own materials. Obviously, there's a huge market out there for desktop publishers who are interested in setting up books for others.

Do I have dreams for the future? Absolutely! Among the first hundred are: putting "Press on the Desk" into book format; writing and publishing a book about twins (not only did we live on "Twins Row," a street with *nine* sets including mine, but also one of my daughters recently adopted a set of twin girls from Korea); adding to my line of business books by dropshipping those of other writers; and purchasing an optical scanner to expand my graphics capabilities. (First thing I'd do with that would be to design Possibilities' first full-color, slick catalog!)

I will consider myself a financial success when my book sales surpass self-publisher Robert Lawrence Holt's. He's the self-publisher who wrote *Hemorrhoids: A Cure & Preventive*, a little book which sold out both its first and second printings almost immediately. What more could a self-publisher want?

"I believe people are divided into two groups: those who prize security above all, and those who thrive on challenge. If you belong to the first group, you could find the the feast-and-famine life of an entrepreneur terrifying."

"To survive, you'll need a strong measure of independence, self-discipline and drive; the flexibility to cope with inevitable changes in your plans; creativity—as in being able to come up with multiple solutions for problems; and extraordinary confidence in yourself and your idea. You'll need the latter because, unfortunately, there are "dream destroyers" out there who will do their utmost to discourage you."

"Join a group of your peers. Their support will sustain you."

Rita Ramacci
Ramacci Creative Clothing

Rita Ramacci says no one taught her how to sew. "I was into it from the start. It was just a God-given talent." That's why junior high school classes came as a shock. "I had been making all my own clothes for years: suddenly all I was allowed to make were little aprons and stuff like that."

Although she delighted in sewing, it didn't occur to Rita to make it a career. After graduation from high school, she tested her wings, first as a waitress and then as a bartender, before she did what came naturally to kids in Kenosha, Wisconsin; she found a job at the

American Motors automobile plant. If the work was hard (located in a pit under the cars, she turned valves all day with an air gun), the automobile maker's wages were the highest in town. During the plant's frequent shut-downs, she enjoyed traveling to places like Denver, San Francisco, and Florida.

Just about the time she grew tired of the factory's on again-off again work schedule, a seamstress position opened at a well-known bridal salon in River Forest, Illinois. Rita likens her work there to an internship which completed her education. "It was a great learning experience." Unfortunately, it was also a high-pressure situation, heavy on responsibility and light on opportunities for advancement. "It was one of those family-owned concerns where the only way to move ahead was to marry in or kill one of them." Despite her growing dissatisfaction, she remained on the job.

The moment of truth came when her mother called to report that Rita's sister was terminally ill. "That's when it hit me—my sister had worked so hard and for what? I asked myself, 'Rita, what are you doing?' " At that point, she decided to go into business for herself.

After making all her husband's clothes, she started sewing for friends. Her big break came with a friend's wedding which called for ten bridesmaid dresses and hats plus an outfit for the flower girl. "After that, things began to snowball." A bridal show for a men's formalwear store yielded a mind-boggling order for 60 gowns. "I didn't have any help yet, so I sewed 10 and 12 hours a day." In the end, it was necessary to borrow dresses she'd made for previous customers.

Her business continued to grow and as it did, it began to encompass the whole house. "My husband complained that every room seemed like it had a lady in her slip standing in it."

Rita's decision to move from home base was not a sudden one. "In the back of my mind, I was always looking for a good spot." Eventually she found one she couldn't resist. Above an antique mall on the corner of downtown's main street, it was all windows, making it an ideal location for a seamstress. "In this business, you need lots of light."

Additionally, there were 2,300 square feet of floor space, which she split between a salon and a work room, which contains seven sewing machines and two sergers for professionally finished interlocking seams. Shelves are lined with large, colorful baskets, each containing a, single project. A steamer trunk holds patterns. Fabric seems to be everywhere. Rita says it accumulates rapidly because she's a "fabri-holic." Often, the extra material comes in handy—like the hot day she felt uncomfortably overdressed. "In 15 minutes, I whipped up a new outfit to wear."

Rita's lively personality is reflected in the bright yellow and orange mural on the wall, which is a replica of the logo on her business cards. An ardent art deco fan, she commissioned a talented art student to paint a life-size picture of three women in art deco style on the entrance wall.

She hired her first help (her mother, Patricia Ramacci, and a friend) during frantic preparations for a major Christmas show. "My mother knew how to sew, so she thought she should have a whirl at it. Now she thinks she owns the place. She loves to make me crazy." A grin. "I guess she is one of my best helpers." At the same time, Rita also hired someone to clean her house. "Now all I do is drink iced tea while I tell everyone what to do." She pauses and then adds, "Ha!"

Although she now has three seamstresses on her staff, Rita still does the designing and cutting herself; they do the finishing. Additionally, she has an administrative assistant who does "all the running around" and a porter who comes in to clean. Rita handles the payroll herself. She describes her accounting system as "simple." "I just put everything into a shoe box and the accountant sorts it out." Her husband, George Gordon, a worker at the Chrysler Plant in Kenosha, helps with deliveries and other errands. "He enjoys it."

Rita claims her staff calls her "Attila the Hun." "I'm a toughie who beats them with cardboard tubes. I speak with a soft voice, but carry a big tube. Well . . . I'm not actually physically violent—just verbally abusive. In a way, that commands respect because everyone knows where I stand. It clears the air immediately."

Ramacci Creative Clothing is best known for its stunning bridal wear. Spring and summer seasons bring in as many as a dozen weddings a month. In addition to gowns, Rita designs veils and headpieces for the wedding party.

Then there are prom dresses, suits, skirts, blouses, sports wear, costumes, bathing suits and leotards. Rita also sews for men. On the day I visited, a half-dozen sassy-looking pipefitters' caps in a variety of colors and patterns were on display. "The guy wanted some colorful caps and couldn't find them anyplace." Rita also assists women in planning their wardrobes. "I steer them toward the classics rather than the trendy."

Women's Wear Daily, Vogue, and several monthly bridal magazines help keep her abreast of current fashions, as do trips to the garment district in New York. "I learned that suppliers can be an excellent source of information on the latest fabrics."

During spring and summer Rita works an average of 12 hours a day. At those times, scheduling her time is a major challenge. "I always have 1,400 things to do—in spite of my best efforts, I can only manage to find time to do 1,300 of them." She admits her mother and husband worry about her long hours. "He makes me take the day off . . . with a wrestling hold on the living room floor."

She lists sleep as her #1 time-off activity. A self-described domestic animal, Rita enjoys cooking and working in her flower garden. She also relishes outdoor concerts, walking the dog, and dancing, especially Jazzercize. "I need it—otherwise, I would have a rear end the size of an axe handle."

She looks forward to the day when all she'll have to do is design, drink coffee, and go for lunch. "You know—be a manager. That would probably last a day and a half."

Although she doesn't have plans to manufacture on a large level, Rita is interested in streamlining her operations. "While there are schools in design, there aren't any schools available to help dressmakers learn more about the manufacturing end."

She also feels it would be helpful to belong to a union or a professional organization for dressmakers. "Right now, there aren't any." She adds this may be changing in the future. "During the last few years there seems to be a rebirth in the whole dressmaking area."

Her greatest reward: Knowing she helped someone look her best on the most special day in her life. "I get lots of teary notes. When they say I made their day, that makes mine."

Editor's Note: Shortly before this book went to press, Ramacci Creative Clothing moved to a larger location in downtown Kenosha.

"If you want to make a career of sewing, sew for your friends and neighbors so people can see your work. Working with women is not always easy. Some can be very picky. Different personalities don't always mesh."

"Do just one thing and do it right. Maybe it will take 16 batches of chocolate chip cookies before they turn out perfect. Put on blinders and don't let anything get in your way. It better be the thing you really want to do, because for quite awhile, it's going to be the only thing you do."

"Always do your very best, because, just like a service business, your business depends upon your reputation."

Janey Orr Reed
Color Consultant
Shaklee Supervisor, Public Speaker

Have you ever tried on a gorgeous dress only to be disappointed when you saw yourself in the mirror? According to color consultant Janey Orr Reed, it's probably because you're in the wrong colors.

To paraphrase a familiar saying, for every skin, there is a season. Each season has its own distinctive palette of colors. A typical "winter" is a fair-skinned, blue-eyed and dark-haired woman who looks her best in vivid colors. "Autumns" tend to have auburn hair and hazel eyes and look wonderful in rich, muted, earthy tones.

Soft pastel colors lend themselves to "summers," while clear, warm, bright colors such as coral and sunshine yellows make "springs" look their most stunning.

Janey establishes her clients' "power colors" by draping them with fabric samples in a full spectrum of colors. Although there are some consultants who use color wheels, Janey believes draping is a more effective method. "It's easier to see how certain colors make a complexion suddenly appear older and more sallow." On the other hand, she says, the right color puts sparkle in the eyes and roses in the cheeks.

Janey provides clients with a palette of colors which becomes a convenient guide for selecting new wardrobe purchases, as well as color-coded make-up. Similar in appearance to paint chip charts, the palettes are streamlined enough to fit easily into even the most compact handbag.

Wardrobe consultations are another facet of her consulting business. "I can go through a woman's wardrobe and tell her if something is a 'yes, no, or maybe.' Because I know it's not possible for everyone to go out and buy an entirely new wardrobe, I see what we can do with accessories to make a 'yes' out of a 'maybe.' Fortunately, most people instinctively gravitate toward their best colors."

Janey put in more than 200 class-hours of training under World Wide Images of Beverly Hills in order to receive the necessary license. Even now, she continues to study and recently completed an advanced make-up class under Mike Maron, commonly known as "the make-up artist of the stars."

With the completion of courses in Body Proportion and Illusionary Dressing, and The Psychology of Weight Management, Janey expanded into image consulting, which she says goes hand-in-hand with color consulting. "Now I can help people maximize all of their attributes. Helping people improve in appearance is very rewarding. They feel better about themselves when they like the way they look."

Actually, color consulting is but one of Janey's three careers. According to her, it was the natural offshoot of her long-time association with Shaklee products. As a Shaklee distributor, she was familiar with and impressed by Shaklee's line of all-natural skin care and make-up products.

The first time someone suggested she sell Shaklee, Janey was definitely not interested. "I imagined someone standing on a street corner with a big case of supplies in hand wondering where to go next. But if someone would have said, 'How would you like to take your leadership experience into a business of your own,' I think I would have answered, 'Tell me about it.' "

The subject of Shaklee kept popping up. The turning point was a friend who claimed Shaklee helped her arthritis immeasurably. At that time, Janey was also suffering from crippling arthritis which was steadily worsening. In desperation, she visited the Mayo Clinic, where she was advised to take twelve aspirin a day and learn to live with it. The plucky Janey says, "I refused to settle for that. At that point, I was willing to try anything."

Thus, she embarked on a program of Shaklee's vitamin supplements, which she describes as the "Rolls Royce of vitamins." Additionally, she watched her diet carefully and exercised moderately. Before long, her arthritis was under control, and once again she began enjoying a high energy level. That was twelve years ago.

Over time, Janey became increasingly impressed with Shaklee's ongoing dedication to combatting the chemical onslaught against the body. She began using many of the products; then, in order to take advantage of the special price rates available for sales staff, she became a distributor. Eventually, she advanced to the Senior Supervisor level, which meant that, in essence, she was running a business of her own with other businesses under her. "My business is recruiting and training others who wish to build a multi-level marketing business."

If Shaklee led to her career as a color consultant, it was her multitude of volunteer activities that led to her third career, which is public speaking. The list is mind-boggling. For starters, she is Past President of Wisconsin Federation of Women's Clubs—the youngest ever to be elected; Past State Junior Director of the Wisconsin Federation of Women's Clubs; Past President of Kenosha County Dental Auxiliary; the Kenosha Junior Woman's Club; and the Woman's Club of Kenosha. Additionally, she belongs to the Pleasant Prairie Wo-men's Club.

Then there's the Blood Center of Southeastern Wisconsin—she is on the Board of Directors, as well as the public relations committee; plus four years of service on the Board of Directors for Sunburst Youth Homes, a residential treatment center for troubled youth in Neillsville, Wisconsin. She has also served on numerous Wisconsin legislative commissions to which she was appointed, first by Governor Knowles and then Governor Lucey. An active Republican, Janey currently serves on the party's Board of Directors for Kenosha County. As co-founder of the Alcohol and Other Drug Abuse Council of Kenosha, she serves on its Board of Directors. Finally, she is on the Board for the Kenosha Symphony League.

As a newlywed, Janey followed her husband Kenneth L. (Larry) Reed to Washington D.C. , where he served as an officer for the Loran Navigation system. When she wasn't working for the federal government, she took courses at George Washington University with the intention of becoming a Speech major. After World War II, Larry made the decision to go to dental school, although it meant five years of schooling ahead. Before he graduated from Northwestern University, their first son Jim arrived, followed by Kenneth, John, and William, at four year intervals.

Although she thoroughly enjoyed school and was a good student, Janey says, "I realized I couldn't be a good student, take care of four small children and a big house. I didn't want to be gone all day." Instead, she chose to become involved in community affairs.

Janey began her volunteer work in the traditional Room Mother and Cub Scout Den Mother roles. When things began to lead to the presidency for the Federation of Women's Clubs, the Reeds held a family conference to discuss it. "We knew it was going to be intensive." Despite a hectic schedule, Janey never missed one of the Reeds' four sons' special activities.

One activity led to another, says Janey, just as every committee report seemed to lead to another opportunity to stand up in front of a group to speak. Janey states she's been hooked on public speaking since she was required to give a speech as a contender for class president in fifth grade. "I still remember the feeling of exhilaration it gave me. I've always enjoyed the dynamics of relating to an audience—the sharing."

Before long her informal speeches evolved into teaching adult education speech classes, first in her hometown of Kenosha, Wisconsin; later, in neighboring communities. Next she began trekking to other states (25 at last count) to speak to Rotary, Lions and Kiwanis groups, as well as various women's organizations. She then began conducting speech clinics for Shaklee leaders. To this, she added private coaching.

Booked months ahead of time, Janey credits belonging to the General Federation of Woman's Clubs for a large part of her success. "I'm fortunate to have access to a huge list of groups for potential speaking engagements."

Most often invited to speak on "Motivation" and "Leadership Development," Janey describes her speaking style as conversational and informal. "I always try to include humor and favor the tongue-in-cheek variety." She also adds a touch of humor to the titles of her presentations. For example, her speech on membership recruitment is called, "I'll be on the Committee, but I won't be Chairman."

Of all the speeches she has given, several stand out in her mind. One occurred when she was the keynote speaker for a Hugh O'Brien Youth Scholarship Seminar. Her audience consisted of 200 youths who had demonstrated leadership capabilities. "All I could see out there were these *cool* kids wearing dark glasses. I wondered if I had anything to say they wanted to hear. Being sandwiched between someone from the Milwaukee Brewers baseball team and a pizza party didn't help my confidence."

Neither did the firm directive: "Don't preach to these kids." But Janey had some heartfelt things she felt she had to say about problems in kids' lives these days. "I told them not to let anyone push them into anything they knew they weren't ready for." Afterwards, Janey said she'd remain for 30-35 minutes if anyone wanted to talk to her. "Those kids stayed for two hours. They wanted to talk about things, especially alcohol." At the end of the evening, to her great surprise, she was voted "favorite speaker" on the program. (Since then, she has been invited to speak again several times, and each time has been voted "favorite speaker.")

Presently Janey is considering the feasibility of signing on with an agent. With the aid of computers, agents can quickly match incoming requests with available speakers, saving Janey time spent lining up engagements herself, and making a more regular speaking schedule possible. Another advantage is that agents negotiate the speaker's fees.

In 1979, Janey's husband, whom she considered her dearest friend, died. She says that her despair was greatly alleviated because once she had an out-of-body experience, during which she was clinically dead for eight or nine minutes. "As a result of that experience, I knew for sure where Larry was going and that I would be able to join him one day."

She believes that all a person can do is lean on his or her faith during that most difficult of times. "If a person doesn't have a religion, they should pursue finding one. God doesn't leave your side if you're committed to him." She stresses the importance of keeping busy. "You must keep busy. Find a project—start a business. You need something to get up for in the morning."

Looking back, Janey says she has no regrets about foregoing her college education. "My life has been a marvelous collage of educational experiences. I met many wonderful people I would never have met if I hadn't stepped out of my own little world. Learning was and is a constant process."

"Color consulting presents an ideal opportunity for women with small children. You can build an exciting business and yet be at home."

"A career within Shaklee is also ideal for women. You make all the decisions—how many hours you're going to work and how much you want to augment your income. It calls for a minimal investment and you are immediately putting your money into your own business—not someone else's."

"I have this advice for those aspiring to a public speaking career: Preparation is the key to not being nervous. You need to make lots of eye contact and smile a lot. The speaker's prime responsibility is to make the audience comfortable. Even when you are just developing your skills, you should charge a moderate fee. You need to put a value on yourself."

Rita Rosselli
Rosselli Dry Cleaning Inc.

Rita Rosselli has always been an innovator. For fun, she once spent more than 100 hours on her knees painting an old-fashioned bathtub with gold leaf. She then posed (fully clothed) in the dazzling tub for a picture in the local paper. Pinched for money as a college student, she bypassed jobs in the library and cafeteria and instead painted hundreds of miniature ceramic Christmas trees for sale. On another occasion, she designed and sold a forerunner to the popular Cabbage Patch Doll. "And I didn't even like to sew."

Forthcoming on Rita's agenda is computerizing her business, painting a mural on her sister's wall, planning special events for the recently reopened Rhode Opera House in Kenosha, Wisconsin, and possibly working for a Master's Degree in Educational Counseling. "I'm always experimenting. If something doesn't work out . . . well . . . at least I had fun trying."

Rita Rosselli's philosophy is not unlike her father's. "He was always the first in town to try something, and my sister and I try to follow in his footsteps." She notes that Rosselli was the first to purchase a ceiling conveyor which transported garments on conveyor belts from the back of the plant to the front. "Our conveyor was used as a model to show other cleaners how it worked."

Today Rita and her sister Carmela Cairo run Rosselli Dry Cleaning. The twosome not only carries forward their father's business philosophies, they also make every effort to maintain the shop's original appearance. The original marble counter—"cracks and all"—is still there. So is a Cat's Paw clock and one of the first electric registers ever built.

Rita grew up on the premises. She learned how to add and subtract on the cash register. "I became very good at working with actual money—forget those hard problems about apples and oranges. I guess money did something to me."

Rosselli's dates back to 1928 when Vincenzo Rosselli went into business making custom shoes and hats. When he realized there wasn't a great demand for either, he expanded into shoe repair. Four years later, he added the dry cleaning services which became so successful that he decided to concentrate on that specialty. Eventually a second branch was opened in Kenosha, and then in neighboring Racine, Wisconsin, and Zion, Illinois.

At the time of her father's death, Rita was married and teaching school in Northern Wisconsin, so she sold her share of the business to her sister, who managed it with the help of a Rosselli nephew. When he moved to Arizona in 1982, Rita found herself back in the dry cleaning business. By then, her marriage had ended and she was eager to return to Kenosha.

Rita is a college graduate (University of Wisconsin-Platteville) who maintained a perfect 4.0 grade point average and acquired an impressive list of special honors. A dry cleaning establishment with its heavy fumes and hissing presses is hardly the stuff of a college grad's dreams. Friends and former colleagues frequently ask Rita if she misses the teaching profession. "They are surprised when I tell them my work here is as rewarding as my teaching career was. In fact, many of the same skills are involved. You learn all about human nature over this counter."

A "people person," Rita enjoys working with the public and knows her customers by name. She also knows their grandchildrens' names. "Maybe we never actually see the grandkids in person, but we see all the pictures and hear all the stories." She points to a sizable collection of postcards on the wall near the cash register. "Customers even think of us when they go on vacation. I have to be sure to put up everybody's card because if they don't see it up when they come in, they're disappointed."

Rita considers customers the most important asset a business has. She remembered Rosselli's "We are at our customer's command" policy. When a customer forgot to pick up six suits he needed for a business trip to Japan, Rita immediately drove to O'Hare Airport and put the suits on a plane for him. "I got a Japanese silk robe out of that."

Because parking spaces can be scarce at Rosselli's, Rita has a special arrangement with her regular customers: if they call ahead, they can stop in front of the store, toot the horn, and she'll run out with their dry cleaning. "What other cleaner has carhop service?"

Since Vincenzo Rosselli's day, the dry cleaning business has changed drastically, thanks to permanent press clothing. Today's leathers, man-made furs, and clothing featuring feathers, spangles and fancy buttons all require complicated processing. A half dozen Milwaukee stores ship designer dresses to Rosselli's for specialized cleaning. Rosselli's also specializes in cleaning antique clothing and preserving items such as wedding and christening dresses, bridal veils, and ring bearer pillows. Other services include repairing zippers, replacing buttons, and mending hems.

Still another part of Rosselli's business involves yearly contracts to clean staff uniforms for a number of large companies. Rita says such contracts are vital to business because they represent guaranteed work and assure workers of their full weekly hours. "When we are short of staff, the first thing I do is light a candle to St. Jude so that we can fulfill all of our contracts."

The complicated processing requires high tech machinery. The heart of the dry cleaning operation is a behemoth dry cleaning machine. "For what it cost, I could have bought five houses." Shirts, pants, jackets, coats, and silks all require different pieces of equipment. There is even a machine— "Steaming Susie"—just for bodices and sleeves. All the machines have names. "Those names get worse when the machine goes down."

Not only is dry cleaning machinery extremely costly, it's also expensive to repair. Service starts at $65 an hour, and because most

111

repair men come from Chicago, it means paying for travel time. Whenever possible, the staff services the equipment themselves. While they aren't able to lift the heavy machines, Rita says they do know where all the screws go. "I've become pretty good with a hammer. Sometimes, we know more about a machine than the salesmen do." In order to forestall breakdowns, she says Rosselli's pampers their machines like babies. "We cover them up at night and give them security blankets and baby bottles."

Finding help to operate a myriad of technical equipment is an ongoing challenge. "I think everyone wants to be behind a computer these days. This isn't easy work. It takes more than a month to learn the shirt unit and can take two to three years to become a good silk finisher. Some never make it to silks. It can also be a little warm. On summer afternoons, temperatures can climb to 100°. New help complains that it's too hot. Although machines are safety featured, workers still need to be cautious. They also need to get used to a variety of hissing sounds. Sometimes they are ready to quit the first day."

In addition to pressers, seamstresses, and drivers, Rosselli's staff includes cleaners who wax conveyor rails and vacuum all the pipes. "We can't have any dust—that would be self-defeating." The crew is like a family. "We have perfected the Japanese method of employee participation."

Because the staff works hard, Rita and Carmela make every effort to pamper them. Each day, lunch is provided. Rita either prepares it herself in the plant's small kitchenette or has it catered. In addition, free soda, coffee, and sweet rolls are always on hand.

Rosselli's is not an absentee ownership. Either Rita or Carmela are always on hand to oversee things. "We haven't vacationed together in years." Each excels in a different area. Rita serves as office manager, plant supervisor and "counter gal." She also handles orders, public relations, advertising, and the bookwork. (Coping with government forms is the least favorite part of her job.) Carmela, who spends most of her time at the Zion branch, plans the yearly budget and serves as the official Chairman of the Board.

The two sisters have become closer since they have been working together. "Sure we yell and scream at each other sometimes, but then we wind up going out for supper together." They also frequently enjoy brunch together at a favorite restaurant. "We say we're not going to talk business, but we always do. It's good to talk over things out of the work atmosphere."

In order to stay current with the latest innovations in the dry cleaning field, Rita and Carmela attend yearly conventions in Chicago, San Francisco, and Las Vegas. Because dry cleaning has long been a male-dominated field, the two sisters were routinely ignored for years . "Thankfully, attitudes have changed."

Regarding her future plans, Rita has this to say: "I'll have to be reincarnated because, even if I live to be 99, there isn't going to be time to do everything I want to do. Even when you are in your seventies and eighties, you have to have dreams. No dream is outrageous. Without dreams, there wouldn't be any reality."

*"Our father had a philosophy and we've fol-
lowed it: "Get the best equipment for your money,
don't count hours—it's better to be a workaholic
than an alcoholic. Give your employees constant
encouragement and show your appreciation for
what they do. Be very honest. If you don't know
something, don't be ashamed to ask for help.
People can spot a phony right away."*

*"Most important of all, have the confidence
to say 'Yes, I can make it.' Be very proud of what
you are setting out to do no matter what it is you
are doing."*

Diane Serpe
Video Express

Video distributors have kiddingly dubbed Kenosha, Wisconsin "the video capital of the world," because that community has more video stores per capita than any in the country. Not only does Kenosha have a glut of video stores, when Diane and John Serpe decided to go into the video business in 1983, there was a growing list of video stores that had already failed. With this less-than-promising scenario, why, then, did the Serpes proceed to go into the video business? More amazingly, how have they managed to make Video Express one of the most successful video stores in town?

For one reason, the Serpes didn't blindly plunge into the business the way many of their counterparts did. "Some people thought they would make a million dollars right away." Months were spent researching because they weren't sure if it was a fad or not. Then too, they heard competition was intense. "We were told it's a cut-throat business."

Additionally, the Serpes knew that if they were to succeed

they would need an edge. On their rounds of video stores (part of their research effort), they observed that many clerks were uninterested—even curt or rude. "We planned to be different. At our store, we'd make a point of remembering customers' names and using them. It would be the kind of place where people would feel free to chat." John inserts, "Actually, we're kind of like bartenders that way."

Research also pointed out that location is the key in the video business. From the beginning, the Serpes zeroed in on Kenosha's north side—at the time, video stores were few and far between on that end of town. "We drove through the area a hundred times looking for a spot to rent." The day John heard a northside laundry and dry cleaners had more space than they needed, he was off and running. By the end of the day, the Serpes were the proud tenants of 450 square feet—just enough for a small video store. (This expanded to 1,000 when the laundry moved.)

If the northside location gave them an edge in the beginning, that's no longer the case. In the past few years, other video stores have opened in the area. A nearby supermarket and gas station now also offer tapes for rent. However, thus far, the Serpes haven't felt a ripple in their brisk business. They credit continuing success to a number of things.

Video Express is the only video store in Kenosha with a drive-through express window. "People come in bikinis and pajamas—whatever. During the winter, all returns are through our window." Video Express is also unique in that customers can reserve tapes by phone. Additionally, the store's self-help arrangement lends itself to browsing. Another bonus is the computerized listings of tapes the Serpes regularly issue to customers. Finally, there's ample parking. "In this business, you have to have it. There's no use starting without it."

Diane went on to say that one reason video stores fail is that owners don't realize the necessity of constantly adding new tapes to their inventory. As of this writing, Video Express has roughly 2,000 tapes in stock. They pride themselves on owning mostly quality tapes. "Some places fill in their stock with lots of cheaper tapes." John adds, "We believe you can only fool the public for a short time in video—people can tell if you are a place that carries major titles or a lot of second-rate things."

If the Serpes had many questions and concerns about the video business, local lending institutions had even more. "Banks treated this like a 'fad' business—they were leery to the extreme."

Upon learning a cosigner would be necessary for a loan, John's parents were willing to back them. While John and Diane were grateful for the show of support, they didn't want John's parents to become financially involved. "We wanted to do this on our own." So they sold their home in order to back the loan themselves. (It was two years before they felt ready to purchase another.

Days, they supervised the construction and installation of specially constructed wood shelves. (Partial to the "country look," Diane was adamant: she wanted wood, not the standard metal racks). Nights, they stayed awake until 2:00 A.M. discussing a name for their store. It was Diane who came up with Video Express. "Express seemed right, because that's the kind of service we planned to give with our drive-through window, self-help system, and reservations taken over the phone."

After "playing store" with the cash register for two weeks, the Serpes opened for business on Halloween, 1983. Both sets of parents were on hand to provide moral support. Diane says, "We were petrified." Happily, moral support wasn't needed. The Serpes, who now have thousands of customer names on file, say they could tell they were accepted right away. "It just clicked! It was like people were waiting for us to open. Fifty to sixty people came in and most of them have turned out to be great customers." For weeks afterwards, the twosome says they were in a bit of a daze. "We kept looking at each other and saying, 'We have our own store!' We just couldn't believe it."

Duties are shared equally, although each has areas of expertise. As "lay-out specialist," it's Diane who decides where shelves should be moved, where movie ad posters and large cardboard mobiles should be hung, and where the nearly life-sized cut-outs of movie monsters and heroes should stand. "We move things around so much, our customers tease us. In the middle of the night, one of us will suddenly wake up and say, 'Do you think we should move this rack over there?' "

She is also the official sign-maker and decorator, her touch apparent in the decorative wooden flowers she painted and then arranged on ruffled doilies here and there. John is the problem-solver and also tends to most of the supervisory matters.

New tape selection is a team endeavor; if son John is home, he also joins them. They review offerings in each category: drama, western, war, comedy, science fiction, horror, musicals, family, classics, adventure, and most recently, "how to" tapes, which are becoming increasingly popular. Everyone gives input before decisions are made on selections.

Diane says, "We do a lot of soul-searching when ordering. We won't purchase any tapes we find morally offensive." Sometimes this involves making decisions which will lose thousands of potential dollars. "We'd rather lose money than carry something like that horrible movie about Santa Claus or that documentary about killing and maiming people." Diane is so concerned about what children watch that she makes it a policy to call the parents for permission if a youngster wants to take out an *R* movie. "When I say I'm going to do that, they usually change their minds."

Tape ordering sessions also include heavy discussion on the number of copies of each tape to order. In order to satisfy customer demand, it's necessary to carry multiple copies of very popular tapes—in some cases, as many as 17.

Despite multiple copies, video stores are hard-pressed to keep up with demand for new titles, making it particularly aggravating when these tapes aren't returned on time. "There are people who don't recognize video as a legitimate business. When they rent something like a posthole digger, they wouldn't think of returning it late, because they know they'd have to pay a fine. Here, they'll try to weasle out of it by sending the tape back with the kids."

John says Diane often plays the heavy in these cases. Once, she chased after a girl shouting, "You're not very considerate," only to be confronted by the girl's 200-plus-pounds mother. Diane, who weighs 115 on her "bad days," admits she asked herself, "What am I doing?" when she saw there was a whole carload of people with the woman. Thanks to people like this, the Serpes, who are owed about $1,000 in outstanding late charges, reluctantly established a policy: *If you don't pay, you can't rent.*

Because the problem of late returns is widespread, video stores have banded together to form associations in order to protect themselves. The Kenosha Video Association was established in 1987. The first thing the group did was compile and publish a "Rental Risk" list which is updated monthly. Not surprisingly, some names show up on everyone's list. "Now if someone unfamiliar comes in, we can look at the list and say, 'You owe money to such and such a store. Before you can take out a tape, you have to pay those late charges.' The party has the option of paying the fine at either store."

In some cases, it may be necessary to go a step further. Standard policy is mailing a form letter advising the guilty party that a claim will be filed in small claims court and that the guilty party will be held responsible for all court costs. Diane points out that these facts are stated in the standard agreement every renter signs when they check out a tape at any video store.

Another problem in the video business is that it's seasonal. "Spring is the slowest season because people are busy planting and doing yard work. Summer picks up because children are home from school and watching videos is high on their list of favorite activities.

"Weather has a definite impact on this business—we're the only people who pray for rain and bad weather. When it's snowing and terrible outside, we say 'Thank God!' We can check the golf course from here. If we see lots of cars, we know we can forget it. But, if there are only a few, we know it's going to be a good day."

Unlike most businesses, Video Express is open weekends and holidays. In fact, Christmas may be the busiest day of the year. "Everyone wants a tape to watch—it's like it's become a part of the holiday celebration."

In four years time, Video Express was closed once—the day of a heavy snow storm. The Serpes, who managed to get to the store in a Jeep, spent several hours calling all 200 people who checked out tapes and told them to keep them an extra night—no charge. "We didn't want our customers breaking their necks."

Advertising decisions are also mutual. In addition to participating in the video association's joint advertising program—"We all know everybody patronizes more than one video store anyway"—they hold "red dot" specials when every tape marked with a red dot can be rented for a reduced price.

Although the public-spirited Serpes frequently donate gift certificates to local causes as well as sponsor a bowling team, they had to draw the line on advertising in area event programs. "There just are too many of them. The public isn't aware of what a drain this can be on a small business."

Diane estimates both she and John put in sixty-some hours a week. They could put in more, but prefer to give extra hours to their children. "It gives them a chance to make a little money." True to his word, son John helped on a regular basis until he entered college. High-school-age Carolyn works 10-14 hours a week, and recently pre-teen Angela began handling movie returns on Saturday and Sunday mornings. Additionally, they employ two part-time workers.

After nearly five years of working together, Diane and John wouldn't have it any other way. (The youthful looking couple has been married nineteen years.) People frequently wonder out loud how they can spend so much time together. Diane says, "I guess we just click. We do everything together—even at home."

Diane relishes setting her own hours. "Sometimes on the spur of the moment, I just say, 'Okay, this house has been left alone long enough—today, I'm going to stay home and clean.'" Another time she took three days off to hold a rummage sale.

When not at the store, she enjoys crafts and gardening and loves to cook. Recently, the Serpes took up walking—it's one more thing they enjoy doing together.

Then, of course, they enjoying discussing their "dream" store. "Going to it would be more than just a trip to pick out a tape. It would be an experience—an event." Based on the Serpes past performance, Kenosha video fans can look forward to it.

"If you dream of working for yourself, try it or you will regret it. Running your own business is kind of like having a baby—it's hard to get away from it. If you really want success, there's never a time when you're not thinking about it."

Adelaide Swartz
Realtor/Appraiser

Recently Bear Realty ran an ad in the *Kenosha News* to acknowledge their "Million Dollar Club." The full-page display featured pictures of more than 50 realtors; of those, more than half were women.

That's a far cry from 1961 when Adelaide Swartz became a real estate salesman. Yes, she considers herself a sales*man*—to her, this is a definition of a profession, not a sex designation. At that time, there were only six women in the city of Kenosha who worked in real estate. Of those, four worked in family-run businesses. The other two complained they were treated like second class citizens in the agencies where they worked. Unlike the men on the staff, they weren't provided with either office facilities or staff support.

Adelaide believes she was fortunate to work under I. J. Bear. "He was one of the first equal opportunity employers around and saw to it that I had the same advantages as the other salesmen."

If Mr. Bear was open-minded for the times, Adelaide recalls that some of the men on the staff treated her as if she were the office secretary. "Everything I did was closely scrutinized. It was as if they didn't expect me to take my work seriously." Remarks such as, "Why don't you stay home?" or "Don't you love your husband?" were routine.

Not only did she have to convince coworkers she knew what she was doing, she also had to convince potential clients. When she approached people for the first time, it wasn't uncommon to be told firmly, "I want a man—not a woman." Adelaide states that things became easier when Bear hired another woman in 1966.

"Educate yourself," tops the list of advice Adelaide offers to women considering entering a male-dominated field. "You'll need to know more than a man does. Don't go in looking for a fight. You have to learn to let some things go. Stay away from confrontations and wait until you have all the facts and expertise necessary. Even then, give the other person an opportunity to save face so no one will be out to get you. Treat your competitors like you want them to treat you."

One reason there were so few women in the real estate field, according to Adelaide, is that only married women could consider it as a profession. "You didn't dare think of it unless you had another paycheck to back you up. Now the majority of women in the field are totally self-supporting."

Becoming a real estate broker was more by accident than design. Adelaide, who was once a tacking machine operator at a plant which manufactured mattresses, enjoyed taking classes at the local Vocational School in her spare time. "The courses were only $3 —if you finished you received your $3 back." She took everything from making lampshades to income tax preparation. Just as she ran out of new classes to take, an ad for a three-month Real Estate School caught her eye. "I thought it was just another course." This time she didn't get her $3 fee back; instead she received a license.

If her husband Richard hadn't mentioned Adelaide's license to an acquaintance of his who happened to work at I. J. Bear, perhaps things would have proceeded no further. However, when she was flatly informed I. J. Bear would never hire her, Adelaide took up the challenge. "I like challenges." Thus she interviewed and was hired for what she thought would be a part-time job. "Our children were six and seven years old at the time, so part-time work was all I felt I could handle."

As Adelaide's hours increased, scheduling family activities was sometimes a problem. "Because I worked evenings and weekends I never could become involved in Girl Scouts or being a Den Mother, but somehow I managed the Home and School Program."

Adelaide recalls one of her first major sales. "It was for a newly built home and the payments were going to be $120 a month. I was so concerned about someone paying that kind of money that I advised them to go home and think about it carefully for a few days."

There have been many changes during the 27 years Adelaide has been selling real estate. A major one is that the general public is more knowledgeable about real estate today.

Years ago, it was standard procedure for a young couple to bring an older family member along to give them advice. "We knew the older man would head straight for the basement to check out the pipes and furnace. We used to call those 'Uncle Louie' appointments." She notes that today's young home-buyers are not only more independent, they're also more educated. "They realize a house is more than a roof over their heads, that it's a major investment."

Another change is the fact that the woman's wages are taken into account when financing a home. "Ten years ago everything hinged on the man's wages. That made it extremely difficult for a single woman to purchase a home. Now single women are considered prime customers."

Problems with racism decreased drastically in the 1980's. "Having a minority family move into the neighborhood doesn't throw people into a panic anymore."

Adelaide advises both buyers and sellers to interview several agents to check out their backgrounds before contracting with one. "Inquire about qualifications and how much time they spend in real estate. Ask yourself: 'Do I want someone who's only in this part-time?' "

She went on to say that there are definite advantages in hiring a realtor to handle the sale of your home. "A realtor will put a realistic, not an emotional, value on your house. They already have numerous contacts with potential buyers. Also, the homeowner often doesn't know the mechanics of selling real estate, such as determining the buyer's financial means to purchase. It's easier for a realtor to determine the buyer's qualifications. They also know how to get the necessary financing."

Additionally, a realtor should also be considered for safety purposes. "As a seller, you open your home up and expose yourself to others. There are weirdos out there. Realtors have means of checking authenticity."

A realtor does far more than show houses and collect juicy commissions. For example, it's sometimes necessary to motivate untidy homeowners to clean up the premises. As a fledgling realtor, Adelaide found this to be one of the most difficult challenges of her new profession. Eventually, she developed her own technique. "I suggest they pick up before I show the house, because that way the rooms will look larger."

In 1982, Adelaide was appointed "Realtor of the Year," which is an award based on accomplishments in real estate and community involvement. Her record is impressive: President of the Kenosha Board of Realtors; Commissioner with Kenosha's Redevelopment Authority since it began in 1981; Block Grant Program; Transit Commission; United Way; the Blood Drive; Vice President of Kenosha Women's Network; Allon League; and the Italian American Society. In addition to all this, she earned her GRI (Graduate Realtors Institute) by attending school for one week for three years in succession and then taking an exam at the end of each session.

Not only that. In 1967, she added "appraiser" to her list of credentials. As an appraiser she measures the market in terms of supply and demand, and economic conditions, both local and nationwide. Most realtors do a limited amount of appraising. When the major lending institutions in the community began to give her the bulk of their assignments, she began to take appraising as seriously as her work in real estate and proceeded to "go to school again," this time for appraisal courses. These days 90% of her hours are spent as an appraiser and about 10% as a real estate broker.

Does she bring her appraiser's eye into everyday life? Definitely. "At one time, when I entered someone's home, the first thing I'd notice was how it was decorated. Now I pay more attention to things like the neighborhood and the school district involved. Then I start thinking in terms of resale value."

Adelaide points out that the life of a realtor can get hectic. "The phone is a constant interruption. Sometimes appointments are only two hours apart. It's difficult getting away for more than a day at a time." When the Swartz's sold their vacation home, Adelaide says she regretted not being able to spend more time there.

When Richard, her husband of 41 years, retired from the phone company in 1986, Adelaide decided it was time to indulge in her first love, which is travel. The Swartzes have been all over the United States and Canada. After a trip to Italy two years ago, she is looking forward to more trips abroad. Also to spending more time in California with son Mark and his family. (Daughter Joan lives in Kenosha.)

Adelaide says her career has many satisfactions. "I get a warm feeling when I sell someone their first home or when people are repeat clients. I have also met some wonderful people, both clients and people in the real estate field, who have become my friends."

"The number one quality a successful real estate broker should have is discipline. If you don't have time-management skills, you will soon get sidetracked. You have to learn how to squeeze things in. Good salespeople don't talk as much as they listen."

"Diplomacy is vital in this line of work. You need to be flexible and adapt to people. By that, I mean you have to forget your own home and standards and be aware of where the seller is coming from. You have to remember, this is their home."

"It helps to have a nest egg to fall back on; otherwise there will be times you'll go hungry. There's no insurance, paid vacations or holidays. You're responsible for paying your own social security and income taxes. Everything comes from that commission. There are lots of ups and downs, no predictables."

Pat Zuzinec
Design Connections

Pat Zuzinec's interests are as varied as one of her intricately woven, multicolored tapestries. Best known for her stunning church tapestries, she also designs vestments for clergy of all faiths, custom jewelry, clothing, accessories, and spectacular Barbie doll outfits which are featured monthly in the new national Barbie magazine, *Barbie Bazaar*. Additionally, the talented photographer, certified teacher, and interior decorator is also actively involved in women's issues. She made her first bid for political office in 1987, and was one of the first women in her hometown of Kenosha, Wisconsin, invited to join the Kiwanis Club.

Pat exhibited her artistic talents at age six when she created cute little potholders and managed to sell her entire stock to the corner store. Even so, her mother discouraged her from pursuing art as a career. "She didn't think art would be a marketable skill." Hopes for a career in Physical Education ended with a kick in the knee from a 300-pound student during a high school basketball game. Her godfather, a member of the Sheriff's Department, talked her out of a career in social work. Nursing was ruled out the day Pat saw a huge puddle of rabbit's blood. "Right then, I knew that kind of thing would be too much for me."

She enrolled at the University of Wisconsin-Madison and despite her mother's campaign to consider education courses leading to a position as a kindergarten teacher, Pat elected to take art courses. "I was determined to find out if I had enough talent to pursue an art career. I remember begging my instructors to be honest. I didn't want to waste time if I didn't have enough talent."

With the staff's vigorous encouragement, she became an art major. Not only were her teachers highly enthusiastic about Pat's abilities, one of them, Professor Mathilda Schwalbach, highlighted several of Pat's textile designs in a book, *Screen-Process Printing for the Serigrapher & Textile Designer.*

After earning a B.A. in art, Pat went on to earn certification as a high school art teacher. Although she duly applied for available teaching positions, Pat had another dream. The art bug had bitten and bitten hard. Enamored with working with textiles, Pat decided to check out the textile market in—where else?—New York. Armed with a thick portfolio and lots of bravado, she visited a specialized agency for artists and designers, only to be informed her portfolio was insufficient. Adding to it meant remaining in New York. "It was so expensive, I soon ran out of money."

Thus, it was back to the real world and a position teaching art in Green Bay, Wisconsin; to her surprise, she enjoyed it. Three years later, she was transferred to a junior high school which was experimenting with an open modular classroom system. "That did me in—it was bedlam!"

Pat recalls her return to Kenosha. "The war in Vietnam was on, the economy was stagnant and there was no work for teachers." To pass the time, she enrolled in a two-year Interior Design Associate Degree course. During this period she created "Heritage '76," a special project commemorating the Bicentennial Year. The 6' x 8' banner celebrating Wisconsin's excellence in Vocational Education remains on permanent display in the lobby at Gateway Technical College in Kenosha.

Anticipating a full-time career in interior design, Pat began her training as an assistant manager at a furniture store. "Although I enjoyed being surrounded by beautiful Scandinavian furniture, I couldn't stand the slow pace." She moved on to the University of Wisconsin-Parkside and an ad hoc position teaching textiles.

Her decision to become active in the campus ministry turned out to be a life-changing decision. One day a coworker mentioned he was looking for a gift for a newly ordained priest and asked Pat if she'd consider making a stole. Only vaguely familiar with the long silk bands traditionally worn around the priest's neck during services, she proceeded to design one. That stole led to another and still another.

Today, liturgical design is a major part of Pat's work. Since that first stole, she has designed vestments, lectern hangings, altar cloths, banners, and tapestries. According to Pat, liturgical design is a growing field. "It tapered off in the fifties and sixties, but then revived out of a need for artistic people who wanted to create something for God. These things add so much to a worship service."

Pat's fabric collage tapestries are distinctive because the designs combine applique, trapunto (stuffing selected areas for sculptured, three-dimensional effects), embroidery, and silk screening. Rather than restricting weaving to traditional manufactured yarns, she cuts and dyes strips of wool, cotton, silk, and rayon, and interweaves them among the yarn. "This gives the tapestry its dimension."

Major projects include a 15' x 15' banner created for a church in Green Bay commemorating the 500th anniversary of Martin Luther's birthday, and a tapestry depicting Kenosha's harbor and lighthouse. The latter was commissioned by an oral surgeon for the reception room in his new office. Undertakings of this magnitude can take up to five months. "It's very labor intensive. There's a lot of pressure when I work with a strict deadline. Sometimes I have to hire help to keep everything moving at the necessary clip."

Pat contracts on her own, as well as subcontracts church tapestries with Potente's Ecclesiastical Design Studios in Kenosha. Although most projects are the result of referrals, she has solicited others directly. "I keep an eye open for new buildings being erected and then try to find out the name and phone numbers of the architects or art consultants involved. Contacting them can get the ball rolling."

In 1976, PatAnn Studios was a part-time home-based venture. However, weaving, sewing, jewelry-making, photography, and woodcrafting projects call for specialized equipment. Soon the twelve-foot work table, loom, casting machine, kiln, serger, saws, and other equipment filled the basement and overflowed into the two-car garage. It was time to make the move to an outside location. At the same time, Pat christened her business with a new name. "Design Connections is more descriptive of the custom and broad design services I offer." Because of her extensive range of services, it was necessary to design four distinct business cards.

If she wears many different hats in her business, Pat also wears them in her personal life. An active member of Kenosha Women's Network, she says, "That has been a tremendous asset. I've gotten lots of support, leads and business through members of the organization." She's also currently involved with the group's political and economics committee. "Our goal is to encourage more women to go into politics." Along that same line, she served as coordinator for Kenosha County's campaign for Senator Susan Engeleiter, when Engeleiter ran for Senator William Proxmire's seat in 1988.

That same year, Pat also made her own debut into Kenosha politics as a candidate in a race for alderman. Although she didn't win, she made an impressive showing against her opponent, a long-time, highly esteemed alderman. She describes being in the race as a great opportunity. "I enjoyed seeing how city government works from the inside. The experience also gave me confidence and really increased my name recognition. I definitely plan to run again."

Another rewarding after-hours activity is a combination of Pat's interest in collecting fashion dolls and her involvement with the local historical society. After meticulous research, Pat designs detailed, historically accurate costumes for her dolls.

The premiere issue (August 1988) of *Barbie Bazaar*, the magazine for adult Barbie collectors, featured several of her breathtaking ensembles for Queen Nefertiti which sell in the neighborhood of $399. Not bad, for a gal who started with 5-cent potholders.

In summarizing the rewards of being a designer, Pat has this to say: "Every piece becomes a part of you. I find that when I'm working on anything spiritual, I don't get tired. If I'm depressed when I start out, that depression just evaporates. It's as if in doing it, my spirit is renewed."

"If you want to work in an art-related area, subscribe to The Crafts Report. *It will be the best money you ever spent. In order to increase your knowledge and skills, it's a good idea to attend workshops and seminars such as those advertised in* The Crafts Report.*"*

"Trade shows are important because they give your work exposure. When you decide to take part in a show, have someone who specializes in photographing art work for the professional take the slides which will be needed for the jury selection. If you have a poor show, don't become discouraged. You have to hang in there. Do lots of networking and you'll be on your way."

Reading Resource List

Publisher addresses may be found in *Books in Print*. Order through your bookstore or from the publisher. Many of the listed books are available through The Whole Work Catalog. Write to them for free catalog at P.O. Box 297, Boulder, CO 80306.

Atkinson, William.
Working at Home: Is It for You?

Behr, Marion and Wendy Lazar.
Women Working Home

Bohegian, Valerie.
How to Make Your Home-Based Business Grow

Brabec, Barbara.
Help for Your Growing Homebased Business

Brabec, Barbara.
Homemade Money: The Definitive Guide to Success in a Home Business

Byrd, Carolyn.
Enterprising Women

Carter, J.M. and J. Feeney.
Starting at the Top: 23 Success Stories Told by Men and Women Whose Dreams of Being Boss Came True

Channing, Peter.
Scratching Your Entrepreneurial Itch

Chase, Revel.
184 Businesses Anyone Can Start & Make a Lot of Money

Chase, Revel.
**168 More Business Opportunities Anyone Can Start &
Make a Lot of Money**

Clifford & Warner.
**The Partnership Book: How to Write Your Own Small
Business Partnership Agreement**

Davidson, Jeffrey.
Avoiding the Pitfalls of Starting Your Own Business

Diamond, M. and J. Williams.
**How to Incorporate: A Manual for Entrepreneurs and
Professionals**

Dible, Don.
Up Your Own Organization

Delany, George & Sandra.
The #1 Home Business Book

Edwards, Paul and Sarah.
Working from Home

Elliott, Susan.
**Ideas that Work: 10 of Today's Most Exciting and Profitable
Self-Employment Opportunities**

Feinman, Jeffrey.
**100 Surefire Businesses You Can Start with Little or No
Investment**

Fletcher, Jan and Charlie, Editors.
**Growing a Business, Raising a Family: Ideas for the Work-
at-Home Parent**

Frank, Robert F.
Choosing the Right Pond

Gillis, Phyllis.
Entrepreneurial Mothers

Goldstein, Jerome.
How to Start a Family Business and Make It Work

Gould, Joe Sutherland.
Starting from Scratch: 50 Profitable Business Opportunities

Hakuta, Ken.
How to Create Your Own Fad and Make a Million Dollars

Halcomb, Ruth.
Women Making it: Patterns and Profiles of Success

Harrison, Patricia, Editor.
America's New Women Entrepreneurs: Tips, Tactics and Techniques of Women Achievers in Business

Hawken, Paul.
Growing a Business

Hewes, Jeremey Joan.
Worksteads: Living and Working in the Same Place

Holland, Philip.
The Entrepreneur's Guide

Husch, Tony and Linda Foust.
That's a Great Idea: The New Product Handbook

Kamoroff, Bernard, C.P.A.
Small Time Operator: How to Start Your Own Small Business, Keep Your Books, Pay Your Taxes, and Stay Out of Trouble!

Mancuso, Joseph.
Fun and Guts: The Entrepreneur's Philosophy

Moran, Peg.
Invest in Yourself: A Woman's Guide to Starting Her Own Business

Moran, Peg.
Running Your Business Successfully

Olsen, Nancy.
Starting a Mini-Business: A Guidebook for Seniors and Others

Paradis, Adrian.
The Small Business Information Source Book

Perri, Colleen.
Entrepreneurial Women

Resnik, Paul.
The Small Business Bible

Robinson, Joe.
You're the Boss

Shook, Robert L.
The Entrepreneurs: Twelve Who Took Risks and Succeeded

Von Hoelscher, Ross.
A Treasury of Home Business Opportunities

Waxler, M. and R. Wolf.
Good-Bye Job, Hello Me: Self-Discovery Through Self-Employment

Weaver, Peter.
You, Inc.: A Detailed Escape Route to Being Your Own Boss

Wilkins, Joanne.
Her Own Business: Success Secrets of Women Entrepreneurs

Wisley, Rae.
The Independent Woman: How to Start and Succeed in Your Own Business

Other Recommended Books

Anderson, Nancy.
Work with Passion: How to Do What You Love for a Living

Bendell, Leonard.
Payment in Full: A Guide to Successful Bill Collecting

Blum, Laurie.
Free Money for Small Business and Entrepreneurs

Borysenko, Joan.
Minding the Body, Mending the Mind

Broadley, Margaret.
Your Natural Gifts

Burke, Jane B. and Lenora M. Yuen.
Procrastination

Cox, Allan.
The Achiever's Profile

Davis, Winn.
The Best of Success

Delacorte, Toni, Judy Kinsey and Susan Halas.
How to Get Free Press

Funkhauser, G. Frank.
The Power of Persuasion

Girard, Joe.
How to Sell Anything to Anybody

Henry, Porter.
Secrets of the Master Sellers

Hill, Napoleon.
Think and Grow Rich

Lakein, Alan.
How to Get Control of Your Time and Your Life

Lant, Jeffrey.
The Unabashed Self-Promoters Guide

Lauder, Estee´.
Estee´: A Success Story

Levinson, Jay Conrad.
Guerilla Marketing

Losoncy, Lewis E.
You Can Do It: How to Encourage Yourself

Mackay, Harvey.
Swim with the Sharks without Being Eaten Alive

McKeever, Mike.
Start-up Money

Miller-Tiedeman, Anna.
How Not to Make It and Succeed

Moskowitz, Robert.
How to Organize Your Work and Your Life

Perry, William, CPA.
What to Ask Your Accountant

Peters, Thomas J. and Robert H. Waterman, Jr.
In Search of Excellence

Philips, M. and S. Rasberry.
Marketing Without Advertising

Rich, Stanley R. and D.E. Gumpert.
Business Plans that Win $$$: Lessons from the MIT Enterprise Forum

Robbins, Anthony.
Unlimited Power

Robert, Michael and Alan Weiss.
The Innovation Formula

Rubin, Theodore Isaac.
Overcoming Indeciveness: The Eight Stages of Effective Decision-Making

Schenkel, Susan.
Giving Away Success: Why Women Get Stuck and What to Do About It

Schneider, Jim.
The Feel of Success in Selling

Silver, A. David.
When the Bottom Drops Out

Sinetar, Marsha.
Do What You Love, the Money Will Follow

Von Oech, Roger.
A Whack on the Side of the Head: How to Unlock Your Mind for Innovation

INDEX